I0075149

101 Ways to Stay Out of Court

Navigating Life's Little Legal Landmines

SHARI AFRICK-OLEFSON, JD, LLM

Illustrations By Brooke Noa Olefson

SHARI AFRICK-OLEFSON, JD, LLM

ISBN:0692093400
ISBN-13:9780692093405

DEDICATION

For every American who takes it upon him- or herself to be aware, informed, and involved, and, by definition, to play the most essential possible role in safeguarding our nation's Democracy.

CONTENTS

ACKNOWLEDGMENTS

As is probably true for whatever profession or vocation you practice, after being a lawyer for so many years, it's easy to simply assume that other individuals know how to handle life's little legal landmines. But, as I've learned from thousands of reader and viewer telephone calls and e-mails, that is not always the case and, sometimes, just a little bit of information can make a tremendous difference in someone's life. So, thank you to all of the individuals who have taken the time over the past decade to continually remind me of this wonderful opportunity to give back.

INTRODUCTION

I've been counseling average Americans on ways to handle their legal landmines through my weekly NBC and Fox television news "Consumer Alert" segments for more than a decade now.

What Are Life's Legal Landmines

Life is not simple today. We are all juggling more than we'd like, just to keep up. Each of us navigates dozens of little daily situations that accumulate into the literally thousands of understandings and agreements that we will make and receive during our adult lifetimes—and which, for the most part, happen without a hitch. In fact, even without our noticing them. From time to time, however, things don't go as planned, and when that happens, life's little legal landmines get our attention.

You love your dry cleaner…then he loses your favorite suit. That oak tree in your neighbor's yard provides great shade for your barbecues…until it falls through your roof. You've been looking forward to your vacation for months…but the airline oversells your flight and you find yourself booted. You've clicked that innocuous "I Agree" button, accepting the voluminous terms for a new computer program dozens of times…but this one winds up crashing your hard drive.

These and the other daily little legal landmines you'll find in this book explain why even when we're totally innocent and minding our own business, we can still find ourselves in the blink of an eye in small claims court.

What Is Small Claims Court?

Think television courtrooms: *The People's Court*, *Judge Judy*, *Judge Mathis* or *Judge Joe Brown*. These are all small claims courts. By some accounts, the small claims court concept dates all the way back to medieval times, when it was observed that average everyday folks occasionally ran into average everyday situations they needed help resolving.

Nations worldwide have established their own flavors of small claims courts, most with a few things in common: they're only available for certain types of cases, they cap the amount of money and other remedies you can ask for, they fall under state or other localized (as opposed to federal or national) legal systems and thus vary from one state or region within a country to another, and they tend to follow more relaxed procedures designed to be accessible so average folks don't necessarily need to hire a lawyer.

Small claims courts serve an incredibly important role. That's because accessing our legal system has become so costly and complicated that your ability to achieve legal justice is oftentimes a function of your socio-economic status. It's true for civil cases involving money. And, especially sadly, it's true for criminal cases potentially involving life and death. But that's another topic for another time and book.

Why Steer Clear of Small Claims Court

In the U.S., small claims courts began increasing in popularity during the 1960s. Fast forward to today and folks have become so accustomed to threatening to "take you to court" that the accessibility of small claims courts may be part of the reason we sometimes don't try hard enough (or often enough) to resolve smaller disputes amongst ourselves. As caseloads become unmanageable, disputes that truly merit judicial intervention suffer longer wait times and less attention, translating to a "public good" reason to steer clear of court when you can.

But there are plenty of "self-serving" reasons to avoid court, too. Because it isn't something most folks often do, going to court may involve a bit of a learning curve for you, including forms, deadlines, procedures, and terms you may have never seen or heard before. It's definitely doable, but it's going to suck up your time.

That time suck doesn't begin and end while you're at the courthouse. If you're like most of us, you'll be thinking about your small claims case while you're at work, in the shower, at your son's baseball game, in bed with your wife…suffice it to say, even a relatively small lawsuit can get into your head. And drag on longer than you'd imagine.

Also, since we're talking about an adversarial process, if you've had a relationship with the guy on the other side and wind up in court, you can generally kiss that relationship goodbye. Resolving things outside of court, in contrast, can actually make a relationship even stronger.

Maybe most significantly, going to court always involves risk. When you submit your dispute to a judge to decide, that dispute is now out of your control. Make no mistake, courtrooms are not always level playing fields. For example, if the guy on the other side has been in the business you have a claim against for a while, he may have been to court before for similar reasons—experience that can give him the upper hand. In a courtroom, your opinion about the defendant, what you "feel" is right or wrong, or even superfluous facts or information you may have about the defendant that you believe prove he's a horrible guy don't matter. Only the relevant facts matter. To be totally blunt, what actually happened doesn't even matter; the only things that matter are what you can prove to the judge's satisfaction. If the judge feels you can prove the steps or elements needed to win, you will. If she doesn't, you won't. Only the judge's opinion matters. Because you never know for sure what the judge will think, you can never be sure what your outcome will be. Period.

Finally, there's the money. While the aim is to keep small claims court costs affordable for average folks, filing fees have increased in almost every state's court system for the past decade. And at hundreds of dollars an hour, if you do wind up needing to hire a lawyer, sayonara savings account!

Things can get even more costly if you can't file your case in your own backyard. Our country has two court systems, federal and state. As you might suspect, generally federal courts handle matters involving federal law and state courts handle matters involve state law. And each system has its own hierarchy of courts beginning with trial courts and ending all the way up with supreme courts. But most states also have the uber-local small claims courts we've already discussed. Which court your case would have to be filed in and where, aka *jurisdiction*, depends on what type of case it is and exactly where the events happened that created your legal landmine. For example, generally a case needs to be filed in the location where: a contract is entered; the property at issue is located; the event giving rise to the dispute happened; the agreement entered says disputes will be handled; or payments are made. If you wind up having to travel elsewhere for court, that's all the more reason to settle.

Finally, remember, a judgment is only a piece of paper that says you can start the collection process. The other side is more likely to voluntarily pay up if he agreed to the settlement himself, as opposed to having it forced on him by a judge. A collection firm can really rachette up your overall costs. But let's say you go to court, win, and can actually *collect* what you're owed. Doesn't that make going to small claims court worthwhile? Do the math. After all the time, emotions, relationship damage, and cold hard cash, even a win can still be a net loss. And there's a reason for that: our courtrooms were never meant to be a forum for resolving *every* little legal landmine.

Is Going to Court Going To Be Worth Your Time?

Thinking about suing in small claims court? Think again, because the chances are you won't get the money you want.

- Less than a third of lawsuits result in the person who sued receiving the full amount of money they sued for.
- One in five people who sue for money get less than half of what they sued for.
- Over a quarter of people who sue for money get no money at all.[1]

Granted, not all legal landmines can be resolved without a judge, but it's almost always worth a try! Consider the facts. Even when folks do wind up in court, the vast majority settle anyway, by some estimates over 90 percent. And most of the *plaintiffs* (the person doing the suing) who pass up a settlement offer wind up getting less money. So why not do everything you can to try to work it out, and stay out of court, in the first place? And if you need a little outside help, consider mediation, which I'll explain in more detail for you at the end of this book.

What's It Take to Steer Clear?

For most of us, steering clear of small claims court requires only three things: knowing how to spot life's little legal landmines; understanding a few basic legal concepts; and applying simple negotiation strategies, which I will also explain in more detail for your later in the book.

What's a "Legal Concept"?

A legal landmine is just something that happens to you. What makes what happens to you illegal or unjust are the laws and theories that apply. To keep things simple, I refer to these as "legal concepts" but they're also known as *causes of action*.

Here's why a basic grasp of the legal concept your landmine falls under can help keep you out of court. The way the courts work is that each legal concept has steps or elements you have to prove to the judge in order to win. Knowing your legal concept allows you to know your elements and whether you can prove them, which allows you to know whether or not you could win if you had to go to court—which, in turn, translates into powerful leverage that you can use to try to settle and avoid court. Conversely, knowing that you can't prove your elements and win provides you with incentive to settle.

Oftentimes, more than one legal concept will apply to your legal landmine. But to keep things simple, I focus on the legal concept I've seen used to win most often in each scenario I've provide for you.

Knowing Your Legal Landmine

Our legal system is designed to handle *civil cases*, disputes between parties over duties and responsibilities they owe each other, and *criminal cases* in which one or more party is accused of an act defined as a crime—which, in addition to being an offense against the victim, is also considered an offense against our larger community, society, or state. Some cases involve both civil and criminal components. But the legal landmines you encounter regularly, and thus discussed in this book, are civil matters. Civil legal landmines fall into two basic categories, *contracts* and *torts*.

Contracts

You'll find that contract legal landmines generally involve an agreement (aka *contract*) where a duty from that contract is performed by you, but not performed (aka *breached*) by the other side. There are different types of contracts:

Oral and Written: Contracts can be spoken or written.

Explicit and Implied: Contracts can be explicit or they can be implied from prior, surrounding, and subsequent facts, actions, behaviors, and circumstances or from rules that have evolved over time.

The legal concept of implied contracts is intended to make it easier for us to conduct our daily business, since some agreements are so common that there is no need to explicitly express them in a contract. Some real-life examples include your obligation to pay for restaurant meals and bus rides, not because you explicitly enter a contract agreeing to do so each time you eat in a restaurant or ride the bus, but because there's an implicit contract under the law that you will. Because of the legal concept of implied contracts, if someone does reasonably acceptable work for you, or provides you with something of value, you generally have to pay her unless she is clearly a volunteer or giving you a gift. Of the hundreds of thousands of implied contracts in which each of us enters in over a lifetime, almost all operate without a hitch and without us even thinking about them. The ones that go south are our legal landmines.

For a contract to be enforceable, both sides need to have been clear about what they promised and what the other side promised, aka *meeting of the minds*. There also needs to have been an exchange of values, aka *consideration*. To win a *breach of contract* legal landmine, you need to prove that a contract existed, that you did what you were supposed to under the contract, but the other side didn't, and that as a result you suffered costs, damages, or harm.

But there are exceptions. For example, a court will not enforce an illegal contract or a contract entered with a child, an individual who was not mentally competent, or someone under the influence of substances. And there's an important exception to verbal contracts known as the *Statute of Frauds*. Namely, real estate sales, employment, prenuptial agreements, and certain other contracts for longer than one year need to be in writing and signed.

There are certainly many other details about contract law we can discuss. But for your purposes of life's little legal landmines and avoiding court and in order to keep this simple, we'll leave it at that.

Torts

It's not uncommon for folks to "get" the concept of contracts since "contracts" is a word we often use and we all understand its general meaning. The word "torts," on the other hand, tends to sound like foreign legalese that causes a lot of folks to run away. I've found it helps laypeople to think of a tort landmine as all those other things that can go wrong, but don't involve a contract. You'll find that your tort legal landmines involve the other side committing a wrongful act or omission other than a contract matter, aka *tortious act,* resulting in injury to you, your property, your reputation, and so forth, which entitles you to compensation. The duty that's not met arises not from a contract, but from laws or customs.

When it comes to torts, the adage "sh-t happens" doesn't necessarily apply. How the other side handled a situation and the duty he did or did not owe to you is also relevant. For example, did the other side deliberately cause you harm? Did he cause you harm by being careless? Did your relationship with the other side lead you to believe he was watching out for your best interests or put him in a superior position to do so? Or maybe harm resulted from something that was intrinsically dangerous and the other side should have been super-cautious or warned you? In the world of tort legal landmines, these distinctions translate to intentional, negligent, and strict liability torts.

What's the Difference Between Intentional, Negligent, and Strict Liability Torts?

Intentional Tort arises when the other side intends to cause you mental or physical harm and you actually experience that mental or physical harm as a result of the other side's actions. So, to win, you'd have to prove the other side's intent, that a volitional act occurred, and that the act caused you harm.

Negligent Tort arises when the other side doesn't intend to cause you harm, but rather has a duty to uphold a certain standard of care, aka a *duty of care*, that she doesn't uphold—and her unreasonable act or unreasonable failure (for example, by being careless or reckless) to uphold that standard of care causes you damage or injury. The concept of negligence is intended to protect personal safety, property, and, in some cases, intangible economic and noneconomic interests. So reasonableness and duty of care are factors based on what a reasonably prudent person would have exercised under similar circumstances. Sometimes a negligent situation arises from the expectations of a special relationship, such as a doctor-patient relationship. And there's a requirement for *proximate cause* between the other side's breach and your damage; the connection can't be *remote*. So, to win, you'd have to prove the other side had a duty to meet a certain standard of care, breached that duty, the breach is what caused you to be damaged, and the damage occurred. In certain cases, negligence can be assumed based on the legal concept *res ipsa loquitur*, which, in Latin, means "the thing itself speaks," or a related legal concept known as *negligence per se*.

Strict Liability Tort arises when the other side can be held liable for your injury without having committed a wrongful act, as is the case, for example, when the other side engages in ultra-hazardous or abnormally dangerous activities or when the other side's product has harmed you. Basically, society is saying that the activity is so dangerous to the public that there must be liability. However, society is not going so far as to outlaw the activity. Some states also allow strict liability when the other side's animal hurts you. So, to win you'd have to prove the other side had an absolute duty to make something safe, he breached that duty, and that breach resulted in damage or injury to you or your property.

These three flavors of torts can appear in an endless array of situations. Defamation, invasion of privacy, personal injury, medical malpractice, and fraud are all examples.

As you can imagine, there are many ways someone can harm you that don't involve a contract. I've outlined below a few of the ones that seem to arise more often and have a good chance of being settled without having to go to court for you, but those examples are by no means complete.

Some Common Tort Landmines You May Encounter

Nuisance and Trespass: If the other side has unreasonably denied you the right to use your own property peacefully, the legal landmine of *private* nuisance may arise. A *public* nuisance is exactly what it sounds like: an interference with the rights of the public. If you're not sure if the interference is reasonable, ask yourself whether the harm it causes outweighs any social benefit. Your legal landmine may be a trespass *to your land* or a trespass *to your chattel*, or personal property. In either case, trespass may arise when the other side uses your property without your consent. Trespass may be actionable *per se*, meaning you have a claim even if you had no actual harm.

Conversion: If the other side took your property without your consent, depriving you of its use, and then used it as their own, your legal landmine may be conversion.

Tortious Interference and Conspiracy: If the other side deliberately interfered with your business relations or contracts in order to hurt you, you may be facing the legal landmine of tortious interference. A somewhat related landmine is *conspiracy*. That's where the other side makes an agreement with someone else to deceive you or do something else that's illegal.

Fraud and Negligent Misrepresentation: To make things easy, you may want to think of fraud as simply lying. But winning a fraud claim isn't easy. You'd need to prove that the other side lied to you about something important, aka *material*, knew at the time she was lying (in other words if she was just reckless that's not good enough) and knew that you would believe her, rely on what she was saying, and be harmed, and that you indeed wound up being harmed. *Negligent misrepresentation* is a somewhat similar landmine. To win you'd have to prove the other side made a material false statement they may have believed was true but was not, they should have known it wasn't true, they intended to get you to rely on the statement, you did rely, and you were injured. If you can always keep in mind that when something sounds too good to be true, it probably is, you'll probably be able to avoid the legal landmines of fraud and negligent misrepresentation. That's because fraudsters often play off our human nature for greed by, for example, making all sorts of incredible promises about an investment. And, generally, courts won't protect you from yourself.

Defamation, Libel and Slander: Defamation may arise if the other side said something false about you and that statement caused you actual harm (no, it can't just hurt your feelings). If the statement is in writing or broadcast it's called *libel*. If it's verbal, that's *slander*.

Battery and Assault: Simply put, *battery* happens when the other side physically contacts you, including with an object, without your consent, or in a harmful or offensive way. In contrast, *assault* happens when the other side purposefully causes you to be reasonably apprehensive that you will be harmed or offended by a battery.

False Imprisonment and Intentional Infliction of Emotional Distress: When the other side deliberately confines you without your consent and without the legal authority to do so, the landmine you've encountered may be *false imprisonment*. But be aware that a shop owner who reasonably believes you've stolen from her is allowed to detain you for a reasonable amount of time. And of course law enforcement has a great deal of privilege in this area. If the other side did something so outrageous, while intending for their action to cause you bodily or emotional harm, and it did, *intentional infliction of emotional distress* may arise, but this tort is typically very hard to prove.

Again, understanding whether your legal landmine is a contract or a tort and which of these concepts, or *cause of action*, apply will enable you to identify the steps or *elements* you would need to prove in order to win your case in a court of law which, in turn, will provide you with considerable leverage in negotiating a settlement and avoiding court. I've included a handy recap of some of the more common legal concepts and their respective elements for you to quickly reference as you read through the scenarios in this book and as your own life's little legal landmines arise. In most civil cases, you will win or lose based on a *preponderance of the evidence*, which merely means more than 50 percent likely to be true than not true. However, there are times when the standard is *clear and convincing evidence*, meaning highly likely.

The legal landmines included in this book are organized for you into three sections based on when and where they typically occur; in your home, while you're shopping and running errands, and in the course of your travel, transportation and entertainment. Now lets' get started!

---

[1] "Small Claims and Traffic Courts" by John Goerdt, National Center for State Courts.

CHAPTER 1

YOUR HOME, AND LIFE'S LITTLE LEGAL LANDMINES

WHO LET THE DOGS OUT: What *You* Need to Know About Pet Bites and the Law

Dear Shari O, I'm minding my own business, fixing a sprinkler head in the front yard, when I notice Maggie Millennial from across the street walking my way with her Islandic Sheepdog, Sven, in tow. Maggie stops to say hello and, as I turn around, Sven lunges forward, sinking his teeth into my bare calf. She lets go right away, but the damage is done. Four clear puncture wounds dripping blood. Sven's fine, but Maggie's beside herself, apologizing and swearing up and down that Sven's never done this before. One tetanus shot and 16 stitches later, I've got a medical bill for $1,900 I want Maggie to pay. But apparently Maggie's spoken with her husband, Mike, and changed her tune. Now she's saying I'm the one who never should have turned around so quickly and startled poor Sven. Now what? Bob.

It's estimated that nearly 5 million dog bite incidents occur every year in the U.S., and that about 800,000 of those incidents require medical care, so this is a fairly common legal landmine. Sadly, about half of all dog bite incidents involve children under the age of 12.

Back in the day, Maggie would have only been held liable for Sven's bite if she had reason to know it might happen, commonly referred to as the "one bite" rule.

Nowadays, most states have *strict liability* laws that hold Maggie automatically responsible for your medical bill, even if she didn't do anything careless (aka "negligent") nor have any reason to believe that Sven might bite you, as long as you were allowed to be where you were, weren't committing a crime, and didn't provoke Sven. In some states, Maggie could even be liable for other *damages*, for example if the sight of your own blood caused you to pass out and hit your head. Other states limit liability to serious injury.

The bottom line, Bob, is that winning a case in a strict liability state is going to be easier. If you live in one, it makes sense to help Maggie and her husband Mike understand the law so that they're motivated to steer clear of small claims court and settle with you.

Oftentimes, dog bite victims are hesitant to seek legal representation because the dog was a pet of a friend, family member, or neighbor. In those cases, being clear that you prefer to avoid court and reach an amicable settlement agreement may also help you save the relationship.

Some states, however, have rules similar to the old one-bite rule, but will only give a free bite if Maggie had no reason to believe Sven would bite you based on specific information, such as Sven's training and prior behavior. (Suffice it to say, for example, that the owner of a pit bull cannot claim that she was sure Fluffy would never bite anyone). So if you happen to live in a state where liability is not so strict, Bob, Maggie may only be responsible if she knew or should have known Sven would bite.

And some states even require that other factors, which can vary fairly widely from one state to the next, exist. For example, some will only make Maggie pay your bill if there was something she could have done differently to prevent the incident. In other states, the incident would have to occur at nighttime, or Sven would have to be running around the neighborhood by himself, be a known biter, or be over six months old. Even then, if Sven bites you while playing or engaging in normal friendly dog behavior, protecting Maggie, or if Maggie warned you he might bite, she could have a *legal defense* (aka a reason she doesn't have to pay you). Another fairly typical exception is for working military or police dogs. And some states apply these rules to all domestic animals, while others apply them only to dogs.

HARD-EARNED MONEY DOWN THE DRAIN: What *You* Need to Know About Home Repairs and the Law

Dear Shari O, The workweek's finally over. I wake up early, looking forward to a cup of coffee and the Saturday morning paper, meander half asleep into the bathroom, and holy crapper! The floors are covered with water. Looks like it's coming from a pipe behind the toilet, which I manage to turn off (suffice it to say, plumbing's not my forte). I change out of a soaking wet shirt and hit the iPad in search of that ever-so-rare creature…a reasonably priced handyman willing to fix my commode on a weekend. Handyman Harry arrives, checks out the situation, tells me it's a cracked pipe that will take a few hundred dollars to fix, and gets to work. Two hours and $285 later, he announces my toilet's fixed and hands me an invoice on which he's written today's date, my address, and "fix toilet $285." I quickly eyeball the new pipe (as if I even know what to look for), pay him and Harry goes on his merry way. A few minutes later that coffee begins working and I hit the throne. But when I flush, nothing happens. No sound, no water, no nothing. Harry's not answering his phone. Now what? Tucker.

The relationship between you and Harry is largely determined by the *contract* you create with him. To be enforceable, the contract will specify what each party will do for the other, which is known as *consideration*. More complicated work, of course, tends to require a more complicated contract, including provisions addressing contractor liens, warranties, licenses, and insurance, and specifying that the work will be done to code. Written contracts make it easier to prove what you agreed to, ideally exchanged before the work is done and payment made. However, your invoice will suffice as a contract—even a verbal or "oral" understanding may be considered a contract.

To win a *breach of contract* claim, which presumably includes a *warranty* that Harry's work is good, you need to prove that you had a contract, you did your part by paying Harry, Harry did not do his part by fixing the toilet, and, as a result, you suffered an economic loss, namely you're out $285 and still have a broken toilet. To settle and avoid small claims court, Tucker, ensure that Harry understands that you have all the boxes ticked off for a successful claim.

Home repair, maintenance, and renovation is a multi-billion-dollar industry and a fertile ground for life's little legal landmines. While most providers are honorable, sadly some are not. Fraud in this industry costs Americans dearly, especially older folks and people in homes hit by natural disasters such as hurricanes. Be wary of door-to-door solicitors saying that they "happen to be in your neighborhood" and are "offering 'special pricing.'" Other red flags include: anyone saying you have to decide "right away"; "free inspections" that will undoubtedly reveal needed work; demands for big upfront dollars; increasing costs as the work progresses; and companies or individuals who lack a publicly listed telephone number and address, and have no references.

WARRANTIES UP IN SMOKE: What *You* Need to Know About Appliance Warranties and the Law

Dear Shari O, I wasn't shopping for a microwave, but my co-worker, Carl, is moving and offered me his almost-brand-new one for a fraction of what he paid for it. He's got the papers it came with, but not the box (which I won't need anyway). When I get home, I plug it in to cook the "b" portion of the BLT I planned for dinner and turn my attention to a cold beer. But a few minutes later I smell smoke. The inside of the microwave is covered in soot and my dinner's incinerated. I call Carl, but he tells me to call Bulls Eye, where he bought it. The chick answering Bulls Eye's phones tells me microwaves can only be returned in original boxing, in original condition—and with a receipt. But I found a warranty in the box which looks as if I'm entitled to a full refund or replacement. Now what? Matthew.

Breach of warranty refers to the failure of a seller to fulfill the terms of a promise, claim, or representation made concerning the quality or type of the product. Briefly, the law assumes that big box sellers, such as Bull Eye, give and must stand behind certain warranties concerning the products they sell.

There are different types of warranties, Matthew. *Express* warranties—in which the seller states facts about the product or service, or gives you a written description or a sample—are arguably part of the reason you decide to buy a certain product. Express warranties can be written or verbal.

In contrast, *implied* warranties are based on factors, including sale circumstances (such as what you tell the seller about why you're buying something or what you plan to use it for), from which you assume certain things about whatever it is you're buying. So implied warranties don't have to be explicitly written or even stated.

But there's another important facet here. Product liability is the area of law in which manufacturers, distributors, suppliers, retailers, and others who make products available to the public are generally held responsible for the injuries those products cause.

In product liability cases we often see the terms *strict liability*, which essentially means liability resulting without the need to have intentionally or negligently done or not done anything. Matthew, if you're able to prove the microwave was defective, and the defect rendered it unreasonably dangerous and proximately caused you injury, you'd have a good case for product liability here. In fact, even injured guests, bystanders, and others may be entitled to damages caused by the product. And responsibility can be extended to vendors, manufacturer—virtually everyone in the chain.

Product liability cases are the ones you often see being handled as *class action* lawsuits as they can be tough to pull off on your own. But they can be helpful leverage. In this case, you've got a great shot at getting your money back from Carl for breaching the warranty that the microwave worked, which he implied when he told you it was brand new, or getting Carl to help get the full purchase price or a replacement from Bulls Eye and the manufacturer—for breach of the express warranty that presumably came with the microwave, or product liability. I'd start with Carl and offer to go with him to speak with Bulls Eye management since he was the legal buyer of the microwave.

IT'S MY PARTY…: What *You* Need to Know about Noisy Neighbors and the Law

Dear Shari O, Despite way too many boxes and a flat tire en route, moving into our new home was among the happiest days of my life. We've got so much more room now and the neighbors are right out of a Mister Roger's Neighborhood *episode. That is, except for Norman, the guy who owns the house directly next door. The realtor claims she had no idea that he lives in Brazil and rents the house on airBNB. Every weekend's a party. I've tried everything. Politely asking renters to turn the volume down. A nice phone call followed by numerous emails to Norman, begging him to limit the number of occupants or maybe steer clear of the raving college crowd and instead look for more mature or vacationing family renters. Finally calling the police and even code enforcement. But to no avail. It's 2 a.m. and, once again, there are at least a dozen 20-something kids partying at 500 decibels. Now what? Patty.*

The term *nuisance*, in legal jargon, is somewhat similar to the way you probably use the word in everyday life: it's something that just bugs the crap out of you. But, in the context of the nuisance otherwise known as Norman's partying tenants, their actions need to rise to the level of unreasonably interfering with the use and enjoyment of your own property and causing you material harm (for example by reducing the desirability or value of your own home). Noise, lights, and even smells are some of the more common nuisances that may qualify.

So, in order to win, Patty, you'd need to convince a judge that the nuisance caused by Norman's tenants is unreasonable and not justified by any public good served by letting them party hardy.

My experience is that it's almost impossible to get absentee owners to willingly control tenants. Partially because it's almost impossible for them to do that and partially because as long as they're being paid they normally just don't care. Sadly, the best option may be to make a nuisance of yourself. More specifically, you may need to call in the authorities, including both law and code enforcement, several times, and leave it to them to notify your dear friend Norman with violation notices, in order to get his attention.

On a side note, many local governments now have their own rules for dealing with short-term residential rentals (such as airBNB and its competitors). Don't forget to check into that angle. If Norman's not following the rules, that may be helpful.

But don't expect an invitation to his parties!

Remember that, despite your advantages, Norman has a wide range of defenses to your nuisance claim—some examples: you're being overly sensitive; the noise wouldn't bother most people; there are other causes for the noise; and your parties are just as loud and often.

FOLIAGE THROUGH YOUR FOYER: What *You* Need to Know About Your Neighbor's Trees and the Law

Dear Shari O, Our eighty-three-year-old neighbor, Edna, is one of the nicest people in the world. She's been volunteering at the local hospital for years, bakes cookies for neighborhood kids all the time, and even puts little American flags in everyone's yard for Veterans Day. She's got plenty of money but seems to live, like many from that generation, more miserly than she has to. Which is actually the only complaint we have: she seems to really skimp when it comes to her yard workers. One of her trees is growing out of control. Huge dead branches are hanging precariously. Others are dropping leaves all over our yard. And we're beginning to worry it could even blow over onto our roof. Robbie mentions it to her indirectly a few times and then I finally tell her I'm worried the tree is so badly decayed it might just blow over. Either Edna's not hearing us or she just doesn't want to do anything about it. And then exactly what we feared happens, the wind blows Edna's tree over, right through our living room roof. Edna tells us she has no insurance, but would be happy to "help cover our repairs fifty-fifty," not exactly what we have in mind. What can we do? Sandra and Robbie.

Negligence, which essentially means not being careful, is a concept that arises with a ton of legal landmines. The expected level of care will generally be based on what a *reasonable* person would do under similar circumstances. It can involve an action, such as careless driving, or a non-action such as not trimming dangerous trees, as is the case here. Sandra, proving that Edna was negligent requires a relationship between the two of you, pursuant to which Edna owes it to you to be careful (aka a *duty of care*), that she did not live up to this duty of care (aka *breached*), that the breach caused her tree to fall, and that as a result you incurred actual loss or *damages*.

Let's say that, when you explain to Edna that all the circumstances point to her negligence, she calmly replies, "The wind blew the tree over dear, not me." This response highlights the fact that there are two types of *causation*. When damage wouldn't have happened but for the breach of duty, it's called *actual cause*. When there may have been damage anyway, but the extent and type of damages are reasonably related to the breach of duty, you've got *proximate cause*—which is the case here. Edna's right, if her tree fell solely due to the wind, which is arguably beyond her control, she would not be negligent. But Edna knew that her tree was decayed and at risk of falling and owners have a duty to reasonably inspect and maintain trees. So even if you had not told her, Edna arguably should have known. That makes her negligent. Hopefully, Sandra, you'll find a way to break it to her nicely.

You can trim back the part of Edna's tree extending into your yard, as long as you do so from your own property and don't damage the tree (killing it could cost you as much as three times the cost of the tree!). The same rules don't apply to fruit. You can't pick it off your neighbor's tree, even if it's hanging onto your yard. You generally can't do much about the leaves; even if they damage your property, falling leaves are considered a natural product.

Many local governments have rules requiring owners to properly maintain trees and may even step in if they don't. Utility companies are another source of potential help if a tree threatens their lines. Your insurance policy may, likewise, cover damage from Edna's tree but be aware that some policies exclude damage due to negligence.

THE TALE OF THE LOST FENCE: What *You* Need to Know About Property Encroachments and the Law

Dear Shari O, The Murrays moved in next door last month and, while we don't know them that well yet, they seem like a nice family. Tom's a CPA and Nanci stays home to take care of the five-year-old twins. Even though everyone in our development has five-acre lots, their poodle, Bowie, keeps crapping in our yard. But last weekend Tom stopped by to let us know he'd be putting in a fence. I decide to check on the progress. It's a wooden six-footer, looks nice. We get all the benefits and he's saving us the cost and hassles of having to put one in ourselves. The only thing is, it looks like the last few sections near the back intrude into our yard. I mention it to Tom who agrees the fence seems to "weave a bit to the left," but assures me it's not a big deal. Big deal or not, I want his fence off our property. Am I being nuts? Frank.

In this day of do-it-yourselfers, it's not unusual for a fence, pavers, shed, or even part of an addition to intrude (aka *encroach*) onto a neighbor's property. Proving an encroachment is simple if you own the property and did not consent to the fence. But if Tom can show that the encroachment was innocently erected, would be extremely difficult or costly to remove, and is causing little if any inconvenience to you, a court may allow the encroachment to remain and perhaps award you monetary damages for the loss of use of your property.

If you really want that fence fixed, Frank, and Tom pushes back, contacting the local permitting department might be helpful. That's because a permit is typically required for these types of improvements, and getting a permit involves submitting a survey showing where the improvement will be placed, precisely to ensure encroachments like this don't result. You'd be surprised how often folks don't get permits, and if that's the case, the local government may step in and require Tom to move the fence, get a permit after the fact, or maybe even remove the fence altogether. Obviously calling code enforcement isn't exactly going to make Tom your new best friend.

However, Frank, if you decide to let this slide with Tom, be aware that when you sell or refinance your home, your buyer or lender may take issue and ask that the fence be moved. At that point you may have to eat the cost to save your deal.

Other concepts may also arise over time. For example, *adverse possession* could allow Tom to actually wind up owning that portion of your property he's using if he can show that he used it openly, hostilely, exclusively, and without your permission for the period required in your state (for example 20 years). Tom could also potentially argue that he acquired a *prescriptive easement*, allowing him to continue using your property even if you no longer wish to allow it. While prior cases have significantly limited its reach, after a number of years, the *agreed boundaries doctrine* might enable Tom to alleged that you agreed to the placement of the fence because the actual property line was in dispute, at which point the fence may be deemed your new property line.

A written agreement documenting the terms under which Tom is allowed to keep his fence on your property could avoid these hazards. The bottom line is that being a nice guy may carry unintended consequences for you. So no, Frank, you're not crazy.

RULES, REGS, AND REALITY: What *You* Need to Know About Condominium and Homeowner Association Rules and Regulations

Dear Shari O, My boyfriend and I recently bought a new home in a gated community. We're both huge Miami Heat fans. But when we put out our Miami Heat flag for the game last Saturday, we found a "Notice of Violation" from the president of the HOA in our mailbox Monday morning. It basically said we are not allowed to hang a Miami Heat flag on our own house. Can they really do that? Stephan.

Yes. Period.

Folks who buy a home where there's a homeowners or community association take title subject to *covenants, conditions, and restrictions,* aka *CCR,* recorded in the county public records. It's the CCR, and the Declaration in the case of a condominium, that give boards the right to impose rules and regulations and insert itself in processes such as approving new owners and renters and, in the case of homeowners associations, exterior home improvements.

Proponents of condo and homeowners associations say the groups use rules and regulations to protect home values and curb appeal, while opponents say they can lead to abuse of power or negligence. Though some states have passed laws to address the authority of condo and homeowners associations, those organizations can legally control what you do with your property.

Of course, rules cannot violate state or federal laws, such as fair housing regulations regarding handicap access. But they typically can and do cover things like pets, use of common areas, parking, and for homeowners associations things like architectural standards including exterior paint colors, roofing material, fences, landscaping, signs, and such. If yours also says you can't hang your Miami Heat flag, Stephan, then you can't hang your Miami Heat flag. That's why it's important to ask for a current copy and actually read the rules before you buy or rent to be sure you can live with them.

Find a place inside your beautiful new home to hang your flag. Go Heat!

WATER WOES: What *You* Need to Know About Condominium Association Repair Responsibilities

Dear Shari O, Last year Brian and I bought in a condominium that's only a few years old. The person we bought from never lived here full-time, so our unit looked brand new. But six months later, one of our windows leaked while we were away visiting my mother. The water destroyed our wood floors, which thankfully our insurance is covering. But apparently it also seeped through and destroyed the ceiling in the unit just below ours. Our insurance policy does not cover that part of the damage. Shouldn't our condominium association pay for it? Molly.

Typically, the homeowner's association will be responsible for *maintenance*, for example plumbing pipes leading to units. However, responsibility for certain maintenance within the confines of unit walls, for example the plumbing pipe directly underneath your bathroom sink, is typically allocated to the unit owners.

Exterior windows are usually the association's responsibility; you will need to confirm what your Declaration of Condominium says. The Declaration and *Amendments* contain rules for owning your condominium that, by taking title to your unit, you agree to—including rules for what maintenance and damage each owner is and is not responsible for.

New condominiums typically also benefit from builder and manufacturer warranties for a certain number of years, which may or may not extend beyond original unit owners. Such warranties are often addressed by statute.

As you mentioned Molly, another source of relief is the association's insurance policy. Probably the most common insurance for homeowner's associations is studs-out coverage, which essentially includes everything outside of your unit. The HOA insurance would step in for incidents regarding the basic building, for example if hail damaged the roof, the elevators broke down, or a car crashed into the lobby. That would leave you in charge of everything inside your unit, including structural elements such as walls, fixtures, flooring, and cabinets. Some homeowners associations, however, offer all-in coverage. This protects the basic building and common areas *plus* the structural elements and fixtures in your own unit.

Moreover, water damage may also be caused by *casualty*, for example a hurricane, which may be another factor in the decision of whether the damage is covered by insurance or not.

In your case, Molly, there are several potential responsible parties including the association, your insurance, the other unit owners insurance, the builder and even the window manufacturer, depending upon why the window leaked. While having multiple potential parties on the hook may sound like a good thing, oftentimes it is not. What we see in condominiums are disputes prolonged by a lot of finger-pointing and no one willing to step up and take responsibility.

Water can be a major issue in condominiums precisely because it often migrates from the original unit, causing damage in other units—which leads to multiple parties and insurance policies. This is why reading and understanding your insurance policy, as well as the association's master policy, is especially important if you live in a condominium.

Your best option, Molly, is to read all of the relevant insurance policies carefully to determine whether or not you are responsible. If you feel the damage should be covered by the association's insurance, then you can resist payment—but be prepared for push-back.

In some cases, your association might stipulate how much of a certain coverage you should carry or even which company you need to buy your own policy from. Your condo master policy will generally cover property damage to the building and common areas, including injuries to guests who get hurt in common areas such as the pool or tennis court, but only up to its limits. Depending on what those limits are, there's always a chance that a severe incident could exceed them. If that happens, it might fall on the condo owners to make up the difference and help repair the damage.

One more thought: liability for personal injury can be an even bigger concern than property damage. A few states apply pure joint-and-several laws where each defendant is responsible for the entire amount regardless of its amount of fault. Other states employ pure several laws where each party shares the financial consequences based on its amount of fault. The majority utilize modified joint-and-several laws where one specific party is potentially responsible for the entire damage or injury only if they are judged at-fault beyond a specific level or amount.

A COSTLY OVERSIGHT: What *You* Need to Know About Association Assessments

Dear Shari O, This past fall we closed on a condominium. We use it as a second home, but plan to retire there some day. We were traveling over the holidays so my husband accidentally forgot to send in the $5,000 monthly assessment on time. To our complete shock, we were hit with a $500 late fee! This seems totally excessive. Can they do that? Alexander.

Yes, they can!

It's the CCR in the case of a homeowners association or the Declaration in the case of a condominium that explains how assessments are calculated, and when and how votes for approval are taken—and they typically give the association and board the right to place a lien on the property of any owner who does not pay up.

Alexander, it's certainly worth your time to check the rules and confirm this is within their authority. Assuming it is, pay now, knowing your husband will probably never make the same mistake again!

States started a new wave of laws to regulate community association rules and procedures in the late 1990s. For example, Florida passed a law requiring associations to register with the State Department of Business and Professional Regulation and report details about their organizations, including revenue and expenses.

It's important to review association financials before you buy. Make sure they have proper reserves, and that line items are reasonable and appropriate. Look for a history of owners not paying or prior financial problems. One of the major issues during the foreclosure crisis was that owners went into foreclosure and stopped paying association assessments, forcing associations to raise everyone else's assessments. Since then, I've seen associations get much more aggressive about making sure no one falls behind which, in the big picture may be a good thing.

THE INSECURE LANDLORD: What *You* Need to Know About Your Security Deposit and the Law

Dear Shari O, We closed on our new home and moved out of the one we were renting over a month ago. I've called and emailed the landlord, Larry, at least a dozen times asking where our $1,500 security deposit is and he still hasn't replied. We deliberately went to great measure to leave the apartment in perfect shape, far better than when he rented it to us, so we would not have any issue with him over getting our security deposit back. Howard is angry at me because he's the one who put up the security deposit in the first place. What can we do? Thomas and Howard.

Each state has its own laws, aka *statutes*, that govern landlord tenant issues. Security deposits are the most common issue I see. If there is damage to your apartment, your landlord can use all or part of your deposit to pay a reasonable price for cleaning or repairs. He cannot use your deposit to repair *ordinary wear and tear*. In your case, Thomas, if you left your apartment in tip-top shape and (hopefully) took photographs, it sounds as if your landlord has no legal right to retain your deposit.

Sometimes more importantly, most state laws require your landlord to send you a very specific notice if he intends to keep all or part of your deposit. And the notice has to be sent within a certain number of days after you move out. Missing that deadline or not sending you that exact notice required by statute is oftentimes full grounds for you to demand the return of your deposit, even if the landlord could have otherwise kept it.

As for which tenant a deposit belongs to, most leases provide for *joint and several* tenant liability. That means each tenant is responsible for 100 percent of the lease obligations, even if they're signing a lease together. In your case, Thomas, that means it doesn't matter who paid the deposit.

Check your state's landlord tenant statutes to see how long your landlord has to notify you if he intends to keep your deposit. If that time has passed, send him a certified letter demanding it back. If it has not, lay low until it does and then send him that letter.

It's also worth knowing that most states require that residential security deposits be held in special bank accounts and some even require your landlord to pay you interest. Many smaller landlords don't always follow these requirements so knowing the rules and asking how your deposit was held may give you leverage in your negotiations.

One more side note; during the foreclosure crisis, landlords who were making money on their rentals stopped paying their mortgages; after the banks foreclosed, tenants were forced to move out, and their deposits disappeared with the former owners. If you have any concern that a rental you're moving into may be sold or go into foreclosure, ask for your security deposit to be held in the trust or escrow account of a qualified lawyer, realtor or title company.

BREAKING UP IS HARD TO DO: What *You* Need to Know About Breaking Your Lease and the Law

Dear Shari O, When I moved into this apartment, David and I had just started dating so I specifically asked the landlord, Luther, for a six-month lease. He said no and I wound up signing one for a full year. Now we're engaged (me and David, not Luther) and David wants me to move in with him, but there's still four months left on my lease. What should I do? Eliana.

Fortunately for you, Eliana, most states have special rules that apply to residential landlord-tenant relationships.

Where breaking a lease is concerned, many require the landlord to *mitigate damages,* in other words, to take reasonable steps to rent your apartment to someone else and credit rent from the new tenant (in some cases, minus reasonable expenses incurred re-renting) against the balance of the rent you owe. The problem is that some landlords aren't aware of this duty.

In some instances, you may be able to terminate a lease based on a landlord breach. In other words, your landlord has not performed the duties required of him. For example, your landlord is generally required to maintain fit and habitable housing and provide *quiet enjoyment* of your apartment. Some state rules lay out specifics, such as certain repairs and maintenance or providing water, heat, or air conditioning. Other issues may be based on reasonableness including the presence of noise, odor, rodents or intrusions by other tenants or landlord representatives, and responsiveness to repair and maintenance needs. Not providing these required conditions is collectively referred to as *constructive eviction*.

Finally, there are local, state, and federal laws requiring, among other things, that landlords not discriminate, provide tenants with certain notices and disclosures, and hold security deposits in certain types of accounts. These are some of the most common rules broken by landlords, oftentimes inadvertently, and penalties for violations can be significant. So being informed about them may help in your negotiations, too.

Your lease is a contract with your landlord, Eliana. When you agree to pay a full year's rent, you may agree to pay it in monthly installments, but make no mistake, the amount you've agreed to pay is the full year's rent. Your lease no doubt includes language saying exactly what your landlord can do if you don't pay the full amount. Reading and understanding that is step one.

In my experience, smaller landlords tend to be more open to negotiation. They tend to not want hassles and simply want to keep their apartments filled. For example, you could make an offer to the landlord that he keep your security deposit and that you agree to pay an additional month's rent, essentially two of the four month's rent left due.

With larger corporate landlords, you're more likely to negotiate with an employee who has no personal horse in the race and has been instructed to follow company procedure, which typically entails suing tenants who break their leases. In addition, corporate landlords have a full-time lawyer right on their staff, so taking you to court in a sense costs them nothing. If you're going against a corporate lawyer, you'll be better off if you can speak with the lawyer directly and make sure he knows that you're informed about what your state landlord tenant law requires of him, including his duty to mitigate damages. If you are able to find any areas in which your landlord has not met his legal obligations under the lease, that will help to provide pressure for settling.

Proving that your landlord did not try to re-rent your apartment isn't always easy and even if a new tenant is found, it may not happen right away or for the same price you were paying; as a result, you may wind up owing your landlord some big bucks. Especially with only four months left on your lease.

Military, job, or health-related relocation are also laid out as justification for breaking a lease in some states. Oftentimes, very specific types of notice are required so be sure to check your state's rules.

In either case, Eliana, your luck might depend on the current rental market. If there's a shortage of rentals in your area and rents have been increasing, you'll find landlords to be more cooperative.

DOG-GONE RULES: What *You* Need to Know About Apartment Rental Rules and the Law

Dear Shari O, When I moved in, I read every word in the lease before signing it. One of the things it said was that the landlord could change the rules and regulations. For the most part, the rules and regulations are fine. But I've only been here a month and already they made a change. Specifically, they allowed small dogs (including my own dog, Muffin) when I moved in, but are no longer allowing them. Can they do that? Donna.

In most states, if a landlord changes rules and regulations after you have moved in with a dog the landlord permitted in the first place, your dog is essentially grandfathered in until the end of your lease term. When you sign a new lease, you will need to comply with the then-current rules and regulations unless the landlord agrees to an exception (in which case he may be asking for trouble with other tenants who want or don't want to have pets in the building). The exception is for service animals whose owners are protected under anti-discrimination laws.

Explain the grandfathering rule to your landlord, Donna. But remember that when you need to sign a new lease, you will have to move...or lose little Muffin.

Pet deposits are also perfectly legal. Humane Societies and other animal organizations are a great source for information about your state and local laws. A few more words about rules and regulations: in addition to considering whether you can live with your landlord's rules and regulations, think about whether you want to live without them. Landlords are generally required to apply their rules and regulations evenly and fairly to all tenants, not just you. In most cases, the reasonableness test will apply in determining whether or not a specific rule and its application is allowed. In addition to pets, common rules and regulations address the number of tenants who can occupy an apartment, the number and frequency of over-night guests, items placed or visible from outside of your apartment, parking, smoking, fire, plumbing, and electrical related hazards, noise levels, use of common areas, and trash disposal.

CHAPTER 2

YOUR SHOPPING, ERRANDS, AND LIFE'S LITTLE LEGAL LANDMINES

CARELESS CLICKING: What *You* Need to Know About Clicking "I Agree" and the Law

Dear Shari O, Junk emails are my biggest pet peeve, so I'm very careful to not sign up for any notifications, or solicitations of any kind. But, about three weeks ago, I began getting all sorts of email solicitations for children's toys, clothing, educational services, you name it…anything and everything to do with kids. If it were just one or two companies, I could simply unsubscribe. But it's, literally, dozens. I've racked my brain and think I know how all these companies got my email. About three weeks ago, my cousin sent me the link to an article about childhood education. In order to read it, I had to type my email address into a popup box. But there was no other language or legal agreement and I definitely never clicked on any box agreeing to any sort of terms. And certainly never agreed to have my email shared. I've contacted the company and asked that they stop providing my email address to these solicitors but was told that I agreed they could do that when I accessed the article. Is that legal? Tony.

By now we're all familiar with the "I Agree" boxes, aka *clickwraps*, that bind us to *terms and conditions of use* for various websites, apps, and services. I honestly don't know a single person that doesn't just click it. No one I know reads the agreements. No one I know clicks the "Printable Version" button to print or download a copy for future reference. Presumably that's why, in today's day and age, this is, by far, the most frequently encountered of all of life's little legal landmines. I'll admit it. I only read the terms when I have an actual question about the service or app I'm signing up for. But you should do as I say. Not as I do.

Courts generally don't require you to actually read the terms in order to hold you to them, just that you have *reasonable notice and opportunity* to read them. So placing the terms and button where you can easily find and read them without much effort matters. If you have to scroll through the agreement in order to get to the button, you are able to see the terms before you're asked to make a payment or download, conspicuous disclosures make it clear to you that there are legal consequences to clicking the button, the agreement itself is clear and easy to read, and you can easily access the agreement afterwards—those are all points in the company's favor. On the other hand, if you have to click through multiple hyperlinks just to get to the agreement, not so much. You get the point.

But what a lot of folks don't know is that, in some cases, you don't even have to click "I Agree" in order to be bound to terms—which sounds like what this website is telling you, Tony. If the terms and conditions of use clearly says that by entering your email address and reading their article, you're agreeing to allow them to share your email address with various vendors, then they can do that.

You can and do demonstrate agreement by your words or your *actions*, and that line can, and often does, blur. Sometimes terms and conditions of use can even become binding when you simply *use* a website or service, aka a *browsewrap*. In those cases, the more a site calls your attention to their terms and conditions of use while you're browsing, the more likely a court would be to find those terms and conditions of use enforceable against you.

In your case, Tony, it sounds as if the website provided none of the required heads-up and would likely be deemed to not have obtained your consent to share your email address. To be more certain, you may want to go back to the site and browse around for some of the features I've just mentioned.

But there's another issue with online-based disputes…*jurisdiction*, meaning what court has authority to rule on this case. One way a court can claim *personal jurisdiction* (which, just as it sounds, means jurisdiction over the person) is known as *minimum contacts*. This means that if an online business or person has sufficient contacts in your geographic area, you may be able to drag them into a court located in your geographic area, even though they don't live or base their business in your area. Sometimes if they regularly solicit business, generate substantial revenue, or engage in other regular and on-going conduct in your area, that's all you need.

If you can't meet those requirements, you might have to pursue them in *their* geographic area, which can involve added costs and inconvenience, something most of us never even think about when we decide to make purchases or work with out-of-area service providers we find online.

So the bottom line is, you're probably in the right, Tony. But it may be very difficult for you to do anything about this particular little legal landmine. Which is oftentimes precisely what these companies are counting on.

TAKE THAT BACK!: What *You* Need to Know About "Final" Sales, Retail Returns, and the Law

Dear Shari O, Just the other day I was browsing in a very swanky store on Fifth Avenue in New York City. When I walked in, I had no intention of buying anything. But I spotted a gorgeous sweater on the second floor and wound up taking it home. It was on sale, but still way more than I would normally spend. I was up all night with buyer's remorse and promptly returned to the store the next morning to return it, but the salesman told me, since it was on sale, all sales are final and the sweater cannot be returned. I asked to speak with his supervisor, who told me the same thing. Is this legal? What do I do? Gina.

When you purchase an item from a retailer, in a sense you are entering a *contract* pursuant to which you agree to pay a certain price and the retailer agrees you can have the item.

Most of us have come to expect that if we change our minds and we want to return the item, we can. Our commonly held expectations include getting a full cash or credit refund, an equal exchange, or some combination of these, and retailers allowing a minimum number of days following the purchase for returns with proof of purchase. Little do we suspect that when we buy an item on "final sale," we may be walking right into a little legal landmine.

The reality is that some retailers have strings attached to their return policies, for example requiring original packaging or charging a restocking fee.

That's why most states have laws requiring retailers who do not meet our common expectations to prominently display their return policies. Exceptions typically include food, plants, flowers, perishables, customized items, and items that can't be resold for health reasons.

For example, here are a few examples of state laws. In Florida, retailers not allowing refunds have to clearly say so at the "place of sale," aka cash register. If they don't, you can return your purchase and get a full refund within twenty days….trust me, I've done it. The retailer wasn't happy, but, as my law school professor used to say, "Too bad, so sad."

New York has similar laws, but the return window is 30 days. New York requires that the notice be "conspicuous," which has been interpreted to mean at cash registers, sales counters, public entrances, and on tags attached to applicable items. The notice has to provide specific information on: whether cash refund, store credit, or exchanges will be given for the full amount of the purchase price; the window period during which you can return the merchandise; the types of merchandise covered; and any other conditions that apply to refunds, credits, or exchanges.

With final sales, retailers are typically motivated to rid themselves of the inventory they're selling, for example in the case of clothing, to make room for the new season's styles, so they specifically don't want it back. That's why, in these cases, the retailer agrees to sell you an item for a lower price and requires that, in exchange for that lower price, you agree not to return the item. In other words, you can't change your mind.

Your state law may or may not apply to items you buy online. But federal law protects you with a *Cooling-Off Rule* for items you buy by telephone, mail, or online.

That doesn't mean you have to accept undisclosed broken items. Those typically fall under the *breach of warranty* legal concept. In that case, a retailer would have an obligation to repair the item, replace it, or give you a refund. Granted, an item could be sold to you without a warranty, but simply saying "all sales final" doesn't mean "even if item is broken." The language on the sign would have to also say something like "as is."

While some retailers' return policies may justifiably frustrate you, bear in mind that retailers have a lot to deal with, too. For example, have you ever heard of "return fraud"?

There are customers and employees who wrongly abuse the return process to defraud retailers, creating a need for some of these policies in order to protect retailers. In fact, U.S. retailers lose between $9.6 billion and $14.8 billion annually from return fraud.[1]

Common types of return fraud include:

- Wardrobing: Buying clothes or other items for one-time use and then returning them.

- Stolen Goods: Returning goods shoplifted at the same store or stolen elsewhere.

- Fraudulent Receipts: Using a reused, found, stolen, or altered receipt to return goods; or returning goods to a store with a higher price in order to make a profit.

- Employee Fraud: Manipulation or assistance from within the company.

- Price Switching: Affixing a higher-priced tag on an item in hopes of returning it for the higher refund.

In this case, Gina, I'd suggest scoping out the store to see if the "no return" disclosures signage is sufficient. If it's not, document that with a smart phone video and photographs. And if the store manager still won't refund your sweater, take it up with their corporate offices and your credit card company. Most state attorney general offices now have websites where you can report this sort of violation as well.

BALONEY BARGAINS: What *You* Need to Know About Advertised Prices and the Law

Dear Shari O, I had trouble sleeping last night so I grabbed my iPad and started scrolling through sale items for some of my favorite brands on a well-known department store's website. I happened upon a fur sweater that I knew at once was priced incredibly low so I bought it. But this morning, I received an email saying that my order had been cancelled. When I went back onto the site I found the same sweater, still on sale, but this time priced much higher. I'm beginning to suspect that the price I bought it for was an internal clerical mistake and the reason my order was cancelled is because the store didn't want to sell it to me for the lower price. I always thought that a store has a legal obligation to honor an advertised price. Can they just cancel my order like this? Barbara.

This is a fairly common misconception that most folks have, Barbara. But sadly, for us not for the stores, while the federal Deceptive Trade Practices Act, Federal Trade Commission, and other state and federal laws and enforcement agencies prevent false and deceptive advertising, there's no general law requiring a retailer to honor a mispriced item even if they advertise it. A simple mistake or, as you put it, a clerical error in and of itself isn't false advertising.

Under the law, a contract can result if there is an *offer*, *acceptance* of that offer, and *consideration*. A lot of folks wrongly believe—and this is when we can unknowingly walk right into a legal landmine—that a store's advertisement equates to a legally binding *offer*. And, if we accept it, a legally binding contract has been created. That's not the case. Merely placing an online order, in the eyes of the law, does not mean that there has been an acceptance by the retailer of your offer. And consideration is not exchanged until the retailer charges your credit card, which most of them deliberately do not do until they have confirmed that they have the item you want in inventory, and that the financial aspects of your order, including the purchase price, are correct. Instead, in the eyes of the law, such advertisements are merely invitations a retailer extends to you to make an offer, which the retailer may then accept by ringing up the order and taking your money, or reject, as the retailer seems to have done in your case, Barbara. This is an important legal distinction.

So the key question is whether this retailer created a contract to sell you this sweater for this price when you entered your credit card information and checked out. And the answer is probably not.

Additionally, most online retailers today have wised up and now include plenty of disclosures in their website's terms of use and conditions on the check-out page, and even on the automatic e-mails you get confirming your order, advising you that their acceptance of your order is still subject to pricing errors, item availability, and so forth. Barbara, if you go back and check this site's terms of use and conditions, check-out page, and emails you've received regarding your order, I'm willing to bet you'll find that language.

But that doesn't mean you're out of luck. Even though they're not legally obligated to do so, many larger retailers in these situations can and do honor pricing errors or provide some other form of olive branch, such as a discount code for 10 percent off your next order, simply to keep their customers happy. So, especially if you're a good customer of this online retailer, it's well worth your while to give their customer service department a call. In this case I highly recommend being nice. That customer service representative on the other end of the line is an everyday consumer just like you. My experience is you get way more with honey than with vinegar.

THE REBATE THAT WASN'T: What *You* Need to Know About Retail Rebates and the Law

Dear Shari O, We renovated our kitchen not long ago. The dishwasher we bought came with a $100 rebate form that we filled out and mailed in. But we still haven't received a check or heard anything about the rebate for that matter. We kept a copy, but there's no contact information on the form. Is there anything we can do to get our $100? Laura.

Fortunately, laws have evolved to protect you from overzealous companies trying to pump up sales by offering rebates. Most of the laws focus on the way rebates are presented to you and the way they're processed. For example, some states restrict rebate pricing or require that rebate pricing "clearly and conspicuously" disclose the pre-rebate price. Others forbid disclosing post-rebate prices.

Most state laws require retailers to make redemption forms readily available (some states require hyperlinks to rebate forms for online rebates), give you a reasonable amount of time to submit your rebate, and process your rebates within a certain number of days. Some even require retailers to accept photocopies of receipts as proof of purchase, or to contact you and offer you time to make corrections if they receive an incomplete rebate form from you.

There are also federal laws, many in the form of disclosures, pricing, and practices enforced by the Federal Trade Commission, aimed at protecting you from rebates that fall under inadvertent or unscrupulous unfair trade practices, or false or misleading advertising in general.

Despite the protection of state and federal laws, there are two problems, in particular, that often result in little legal landmines. First, it's still not all that difficult for companies to make it easy for us to mess up on rebates— especially since most of us need to buy the product anyway and don't bother reading the rebate fine print, which then justifies them giving us zilch. Some common tactics include: limiting rebates to online or in-store purchases or to specific products; including quick submission deadlines; or requiring specific forms for proof of purchase that many of us don't retain. The second problem is that, in truth, many rebates are not for huge sums of money, which some of us sort of view as "free money," so we may not try too hard to get them.

The most common form of rebate is what you're describing, Laura: *mail-in rebates*. Companies offering rebates know not all of us will remember to mail them in (retailers refer to unredeemed rebates as *breakage*). Of those of us that do, many submit the rebate incorrectly—which, according to what the fine print normally says, means we get nothing. And for those who do get a check, incredibly many will lose or forget to cash it in (aka *slippage*). All told, we leave between 40 percent and 60 percent of all rebates, totaling over $500 million each year, on the proverbial table.

Another complication is that many companies contract fulfillment houses to handle their rebates, creating a communication barrier that leaves customers, as you noted, with no means for communicating with the company. And the fulfillment house will only send you the rebate if the company that hired them has provided the money.

You should know that the rebate process can take 10 weeks or longer. It sounds as if you are still in that window period, Laura, so you may still get your $100. While you're waiting, be careful about throwing away junk mail—some rebates are disguised that way specifically so that you'll do that and never cash the check. And if your rebate doesn't end up coming, I'd urge you to file a complaint with the Federal Trade Commission or your state attorney general. That may not get you your money, but if enough people have the same problem and also file, at least the company and fulfillment house may be looked at.

THE CASE OF THE FORGOTTEN GIFT: What *You* Need to Know About Gift Cards and the Law

Dear Shari O, My boss gave me a gift card from a major big box store for Christmas a few years ago and, to be honest, I put it someplace safe...and then totally forgot about it. I found it last weekend and decided to use it to buy some new bathroom accessories. But when I got to the checkout, the cashier told me the gift card had expired. Does that mean they just get to keep the money? The face value says $500! Rick.

The answer is...it depends.

Some common forms of gift cards include retail gift cards you can purchase from a specific retailer, restaurant, or other type of merchant, which seems to be what you have, Rick, and bank gift cards that you can purchase with American Express, Master Card, or Discover branding; bank cards are redeemable wherever those types of credit cards are accepted.

Gift cards and certificates are big money-makers. On top of the dollars we spend on the face value of gift cards, the card issuers make even more money by regulating gift cards with expiration dates and by knowing that we're likely to either spend more than the face value of the gift card, leave a little bit of unspent balance on the card forever, or sometimes even forget to redeem it altogether.

From the perspective of legal concepts, when you buy (or in this case are given) a gift, you're entering into a contract with the retailer or bank that issued the gift card. The person you give the gift card to is bound by the same agreement. The problem, and the reason we wind up with a legal landmine, is that most of us have no idea what these terms are. Getting into the habit of writing expiration dates in black Sharpie on the front of gift cards can help.

Most states have laws addressing gift cards. For example, in one of the more consumer-oriented states, gift cards cannot expire and retailers have to give you cash for any remaining balance under $10. The federal Credit Card Accountability Responsibility and Disclosure Act, aka the CARD Act, also regulates gift cards, including requiring clear expiration dates and prohibiting expirations less than five years after purchase. This law provides a baseline of applicable laws for states that don't have their own.

So the answer is going to depend on what state you live in, what your state law says about gift card expirations, whether the CARD Act applies, and what the expiration date on your gift card and terms of use and conditions you're subject to say, Rick.

I've found that store managers can be very helpful, especially when you've got a cart full of merchandise you were planning to buy on the spot with the gift card. If the law is on your side and you still wind up having an unresolvable problem with the big box company that issued your gift card, try calling the Federal Trade Commission or your state attorney general.

Some final advice about gift cards: always treat your card like cash. If you lose it or it's stolen, report it immediately. Since someone else can easily find and use your card, retailers and banks are not legally obligated to replace the value that was on the card.

FOILED BY FINE PRINT: What *You* Need to Know About Credit Card Contracts and the Law

Dear Shari O, I took out a credit card as soon as I got out of college and basically went wild. Fortunately I was able to negotiate a repayment plan with the credit card company and I paid off all but $1000. Oddly, I never heard a word from them about this balance. I haven't used the account in three or four years. But last week, out of the blue, I began getting collections calls from them. Can they do that? I thought this was in the past. Marisol.

The answer is probably.

When you receive a new credit card in the mail it comes with the legal terms and conditions that apply should you choose to activate the card: this is your *contract* with the credit card company. The credit card companies also send you updates amending your agreement; you accept these amendments by continuing to use your credit card.

Marisol, I often encourage viewers to take the time to read these documents. Sadly, although half of Americans read at about a ninth grade level or lower, credit card agreements are typically written at about an eleventh grade reading level. Which is maybe why almost half of us don't read them.[2] Which, in turn, is why some many wind up in credit card-related legal landmines.

So the answer to this question depends, in part, upon what your agreement says. In most of the cases I've seen, the agreements are (obviously) written to give the credit card company the upper hand.

But there are state laws that apply and, in some cases, can protect you. Generally, if you fall behind on credit card payments, your state's laws give the credit card company a limited amount of time, referred to as a *statute of limitations*, to sue you for the balance. The clock typically begins ticking when you default. Some states have statutes of limitations for as little as three years, but in other states the statute of limitations is longer.

And there's a catch. Since credit card companies have customers and offices in many states, a concept called *choice of law* allows them to decide which state's statute of limitation they want to be governed by. The problem is that some states also have a *nonresident tolling exception* that essentially allows credit card companies to take advantage of the longest statute of limitations between your state and their choice of law state. Find the choice of law state in your credit card agreement and then look up online that state's statute of limitations and whether or not it has a nonresident tolling exception. If the applicable statute of limitations has expired, you're in luck!

And there's still federal law. A federal law that often applies to credit card disputes is the *Fair Debt Collection Practices Act*, which, among other things, prohibits debt collectors from suing you after the applicable statute of limitations has expired. Federal rules also now require companies to provide you with an easy-to-understand summary of important agreement terms. And, if you can't find your agreement, the Credit Card Accountability Responsibility and Disclosure Act, aka the CARD Act, now requires most credit card companies to give you online access to your full agreement, even if you're no longer a current cardholder.

ALL WASHED UP: What *You* Need to Know About Car Washes and the Law

Dear Shari O, I've been driving used cars my entire life. I finally splurged for a brand-new Honda last month. As luck would have it, I took it to the car wash a few days ago and, when I got home, my wife noticed a long scratch on the passenger door. I called the car wash and left a message asking the manager to call me back, but have not heard a word. I'm thinking about going back to the car wash to talk to him in person, but want to be sure I handle this correctly. What should I do? Bill.

Car wash-related landmines like yours are not uncommon, Bill. Most of the issues I hear about involve the automatic rotating brushes that can trap dirt, debris, or rocks from prior cars and then scratch yours, and other moving parts that can damage or break parts protruding from your car, including antennas.

Car washes typically post signs advising you to remove exterior items before entering the wash, and also advising you that they are not responsible for damage to your car. The posting of these signs, from a legal standpoint, arguably creates an agreement transferring responsibility and liability for damage to you and away from the car wash. While most car washes try to disclaim responsibility for all damage, in situations like this, the car wash still needs to meet a reasonable standard of care. So, if damage results from their failure to meet this standard, aka *negligence*, they may be on the hook.

But proving that a car wash did not meet a certain standard of care, and that this failure is what caused the damage to your car, is often not easy. Just as importantly, Bill, leaving the car wash and discovering damage later puts you in the almost impossible position of trying to prove that the car wash, and not something that happened after you left the car wash, caused the damage. In fact, Bill, even you can't be 100 percent certain that the scratch occurred at the car wash.

In the future, take a minute to read the legal disclaimers and to photograph your car before entering a car wash, and then walk around and check your car for damage before leaving. If your car is damaged, ask to speak with the owner or manager. Ask for the company's insurance information and a copy of the damage report, take photos of the damage and legal signage, and ask both customer and employee witnesses if they're willing to provide contact information in case collaboration is needed.

Remember, when it comes to small claims court, it's not a matter of what actually happened, but rather of what you can prove to the judge's satisfaction. Not having taken these precautions, it's going to be difficult for you to prove the legal elements necessary to win this case and get paid, Bill. Regardless, it's worth sending a formal letter with photos and an estimate to the car wash owner. If you're a good customer and there's not a lot of money at issue, the car wash may write you a check for the lowest estimate.

TAKEN TO THE CLEANERS: What *You* Need to Know About Dry Cleaners and the Law

Dear Shari O, I'm not a fancy guy. Fortunately I work in IT, which tends to mean casual workplaces, so I wear jeans or chinos and a button-down shirt to work most days. But last month we had a meeting in Manhattan that my boss said required a suit and tie. I have a navy suit but my girlfriend, who is totally into fashion, said the ties I had were not up to par. So she helped me pick out a new one at one of those Italian designer stores in the nearby outlet mall. The regular retail price said $325, but I paid $55 so I felt like I got a good deal. Anyway, I wore it to the meeting and got a few compliments, but when I got home, I noticed a spot on the tie. So I took it to the dry cleaners we've been using for the past few years. Earlier today I picked it up. But when I got home and took the plastic off I noticed a huge burn right in the middle. I called the dry cleaner and they asked me to bring them the receipt from when I bought the tie and said they'd pay me for it. The thing is, my receipt says $55, but if I want to buy another tie like that it's going to cost me $325. Can I ask them to pay me the $325? Stuart.

It's not uncommon for dry cleaners to post signs saying they're not responsible for damage to the items we leave in their care. Notwithstanding the signs, dry cleaners are still legally required to take "reasonable" care of the items you leave with them, Stuart. They can't be reckless or *negligent* with your tie. It would seem that the fact that the damage occurred is evidence enough that the dry cleaner did not meet this standard of care. But I sometimes see dry cleaners trying to pin damage of this nature on some sort of manufacturer defect. In other words, they allegedly followed reasonable procedures, but there was something wrong with your tie and that defect, not the dry cleaner's actions, caused the damage. Similar defenses arise frequently with legal landmines involving negligence.

Proving that the damage is the dry cleaner's responsibility and that the dry cleaner should have to pay you for it is one thing, but proving the value of your tie and that damage, as you've pointed out, Stuart, is quite another. In most cases, the maximum amount of money that your dry cleaner is obliged to pay you is the value of the tie when you left it with them, not what your tie would cost to replace as new. Oftentimes, a dry cleaner can even successfully argue to reduce that amount to the value of an item's remaining useful life.

In a perfect world, you would have taken photographs of your tie before leaving it at the dry cleaners and examined it while still at the store picking it up. But, in this case, especially because you just picked up the tie from the dry cleaners, my instinct is that your dry cleaner will agree to reimburse the $55 you paid for this tie. But the law is not on your side when it comes to the $325 you believe that your tie is actually worth. And I would take the tie back to the dry cleaners and resolve this as soon as possible in order to avoid the possibility of your dry cleaner claiming that you somehow did the damage yourself after picking the tie up.

If you run into trouble getting any service provider to accept responsibility, try contacting its trade association. Oftentimes, trade associations have complaint processes and sometimes even reconciliation processes.

SLIP-SLIDING INTO A LEGAL LANDMINE: What *You* Need to Know About Slips and Falls and the Law

Dear Shari O, Sometimes I help out my cousin Juanita, who has a very successful small business as a seamstress. A few weeks ago I was helping her set up the new shop she moved the business into. As I was putting some fabric onto a shelf that was in the space, the shelf fell onto my foot. I was sort of embarrassed and I really didn't think I was badly hurt. But the next day my big toe was black and blue. And a few days later the toenail fell off. I went to the podiatrist to make sure nothing was broken and it's not. But I do feel that someone should pay for the doctor's visit and the ointment he prescribed, which together total $195. I feel badly asking Juanita because she had no idea the shelf would fall either. Do you have any suggestions? Melissa.

Although more major accidents are best suited for a *personal injury* lawyer and are beyond the jurisdiction of small claims court and thus the scope of this book, smaller accidents like this happen all the time (typically when we least expect it) and can be considered one of life's little legal landmines.

A lot of folks wrongly believe that if they get hurt on someone else's property, that other person will automatically be considered at fault. But, as the saying goes, sometimes, sh-t just happens. People fall, things drop, the world is not perfect. So, under the law, it's not always someone's fault. To be at fault, aka *negligent* under the law, you have to have a duty of care to do something and breach that duty.

The owners and managers of any business, from retail shops in shopping centers to companies or service businesses in office buildings to hotels, restaurants, supermarkets, gyms, movie theaters, and so forth, all have a *duty of care* to make sure their premises are safe for you from *reasonably foreseeable* accidents. Under the law, not meeting the duty of care to make sure that premises are safe for you from reasonably foreseeable accidents may be deemed *negligent*. Some of the more common accidents that tend to occur at these places and wind up in small claims court include those resulting from minor escalator accidents, entryway mats, wet floors, and falling items—much like what happened to you, Melissa.

Because the ownership and management of commercial properties often involve multiple parties, for example owners, managers, tenants, insurers, and so forth, identifying who owes you the duty of care can be more complicated in this type of case than others and you may wind up pursuing multiple parties. This raises an interesting question for you, Melissa, since you may be able to ask not only your cousin, but also the owner or landlord of the shop she is renting (who most likely has insurance coverage for this exact type of situation) to reimburse your $195. It may be worth your while to take a look at the lease between Juanita and her landlord, as it may allocate responsibility for safely maintaining the premises in order to avoid accidents like this to Juanita or may even simply state that she accepted the premises "as is."

The problem is that when accidents like this happen, we tend to feel embarrassed and do not want to draw attention to ourselves. So, as you noted, Melissa, the first thing most of us do when we hurt ourselves in public is to behave as if it's no big deal. But that's exactly when you should be thinking about how you're going to feel in the very near future...the pain of an injury and the costs it entails.

Generally, if you're hurt in places and under circumstances like this, asking for a manager, getting contact information from any customer and employee witnesses, taking photographs of the scene, filing an incident report, getting documented medical attention, maintaining invoices for all expenses, and keeping track of how your injury interferes with your daily life is key. That's because these are some of the things you'll need in order to prove that the duty of care was not met—that the property owner, manager, and/or proprietor either caused or should have recognized a dangerous condition and removed or repaired the potential danger, but did not, and your injury resulted from that breach. You'll also have to show what your damages were. In this type of case, you're the one with the *burden of proof*. Key questions to ask yourself here include: Would a reasonable person in the other side's shoes have identified the condition as hazardous? Was it reasonably foreseeable that someone could be harmed? And did the other side have enough time and opportunity to remedy the situation? In other words, would a reasonable person have arguably noticed and addressed the hazard? In the case of property-related hazards, factors include regular and thorough procedures and efforts to keep the property safe and clean, prompt methods for correcting hazards, the specific reason this hazard existed in the first place (i.e., whether it was necessary for some reason), and the specific steps taken in this instance (i.e., whether something more or quicker could have been done). In your case, Melissa, would a reasonable person in your cousin or her landlord's shoes have noticed something wrong with the shelf?

Anyplace anyone might get hurt—a business, gym, restaurant, or supermarket, for example—is likely to try to show that the accident was somehow at least partially your fault, aka *contributory or comparative fault or negligence*. If your state follows contributory fault rules and you had any responsibility for the accident, you may be out of luck. If yours is a comparative negligence state, the amount of money you're awarded may be reduced by a percentage equal to your share of responsibility for the accident.

In order to determine whether you might be on the hook for causing any portion of your injuries, you can ask yourself questions such as: Were you allowed to be in the area where the accident happened? Did you do anything that might have prevented the other side from noticing the hazard? Were you not paying sufficient attention, maybe talking or texting? Were there warnings posted that you missed or precautions that you avoided or circumvented? Was the hazardous condition the reason for your accident, aka *causal link*? In other words, would a reasonable person have arguably noticed or otherwise avoided the hazard? In your case, Melissa, would a reasonable person in your shoes have noticed something wrong with the shelf?

If you do not find anything in your cousin's lease allocating responsibility for this shelf to her, and after asking yourself these questions you believe that you acted reasonably and that the landlord leasing this space to your cousin with this dangerous shelf did not, my suggestion is that you and your cousin, together, request reimbursement of the $195 from her landlord.

BENDERS AND BENJAMINS: What *You* Need to Know About Fender Benders and the Law

Dear Shari O, I was in what I thought was a minor fender bender the other night. It was cold, dark, and raining. I was driving along well within the speed limit, minding my own business, when a middle-aged woman driving a brand-new Mercedes Benz backed out in front of me. She admitted it was entirely her fault. I drive a 2014 Ford, which has a rubber-type bumper, which was scratched and cracked in two places, but that was the extent of the damage. The Mercedes had no damage. She seemed super-nice, apologetic and rich. So rather than wait for the police, we just exchanged insurance and contact information and she told me to send her the repair invoice that she would then pay. I'll admit I was surprised when replacing my bumper wound up costing almost $2,000. I sent her the invoice as we agreed. That was two weeks ago. I've left her several voice messages, but still haven't heard back and am now wondering if maybe I've been screwed. What do you suggest I do? Paul.

There are about 10 million car collisions each year. Fortunately, most are "fender benders" like yours, Paul, and no one is injured.[3] In fact, we've come to think of them more as annoyances, hence the inclusion of this topic under life's little legal landmines.

It isn't against the law per se to just exchange insurance information and move on after a fender bender. But it's often against the law to "leave the scene of the accident." In fact, some states require you to report an accident, and, if damage exceeds a certain dollar amount, may cite you if you don't. Depending on how much damage is done, some states even require you to report accidents to the state's Department of Motor Vehicles. By calling the police and filing a report, you're accomplishing two important things. You're bringing in a neutral third party witness to document what happened and you're ensuring that you can't be accused of breaking any laws.

And while many folks, understandably, don't want to report a fender bender to the insurance carrier, perhaps because they have a high deductible they'll have to pay anyway or for fear that reporting the accident will cause their insurance premiums to increase, bear in mind that insurance policies often require you to report any and all accidents, regardless of magnitude.

You were wise to exchange car insurance and contact information as this at least arguably provides evidence of her agreement to pay you for the damage and, if you don't hear back from Mrs. Mercedes, you can contact her insurance company.

It is not at all unusual for folks to settle fender benders on their own like you did, Paul. The problem is, we need to treat even informal agreements following fender benders like the financial contracts they are. For example, in this case, you essentially entered into a $2,000 contract with Mrs. Mercedes, but you didn't document that agreement, which can make enforcing it difficult. In a perfect world, you would have had Mrs. Mercedes sign something that at least reflected she was at fault and agreed to pay for your damage. I'm not sure whether or not you took photographs (of both cars and the scene) or were able to get names and contact information for any other witnesses. But those are other ways to help corroborate what happened. At this point, it's going to be your word against hers.

HEALTHCARE-LESS: What *You* Need to Know About Insurance Claims and the Law

Dear Shari O, My kids had their annual pediatrician check-up last month. I paid my $10 co-pay. But yesterday I got a bill from my health insurance company for the balance of the entire $350 office visit. For each of my three kids! I don't have money like that just sitting around. And I don't understand why the insurance company isn't paying this. I've had the same pediatrician and the same insurance company and policy since my oldest daughter was born and they always pay for the kids' annual visit. What can I do? Luiz.

Because, in the eyes of the law, your policy is a contract between you and your carrier, what your carrier is and is not obligated to pay for depends on what your policy says. Most health insurance claim denial lawsuits are based upon a *breach of contract* claim. One of the duties contracting parties owe one another is the duty to deal in *good faith*. This means that neither party will seek to deny the other the benefits for which they have contracted. When an insurer issues a health insurance claim denial wrongfully, they are arguably acting in bad faith.

Annual pediatrician visits are typically considered covered services under health insurance company policies or *contracts*. The carrier can modify the terms of these contracts (because the contracts themselves give them the power to do so), so that policies that appear to be the same may change from one year to the next. Since the advent of the Affordable Care Act, services such as these are essentially required to be covered. Moreover, if you've had the same pediatrician (assuming she is still "in network") and the same policy, and your insurance carrier's been paying for this service for years, my instinct is that there may have been an error made in submitting or processing your claim. For example, some of the more common clerical mistakes that can lead to denial include incorrectly spelled subscriber or patient name, date of birth, and policy or group number.

In your case, Luiz, the first step I'd suggest is to identify the insurer's reason for denying your annual pediatrician visit claim. The pediatrician's staff may be able to help explain the insurer's stated reasons for refusing coverage. If they cannot, you may need to call or online chat with your insurer, which, I realize, can be a time-consuming nightmare. Be sure to take copious notes, including the names of whomever you speak with—and ask for specific paragraphs in your policy that say whatever they tell you your policy says so that if you wind up having to dig that deep you can. And always ask to have your conversation put into the computer record on their end.

The reasoning behind a denial will provide some insight as to your options. The most common reasons for appropriate claim denials include: services or procedures not covered by your policy; a procedure being considered experimental, cosmetic, investigational, or not medically necessary; a referral or pre-authorization being required; policy limits being exceeded; deductibles or maximum out-of-pocket contributions not having yet been met; using an out-of-network provider; or a claim being filed too late, or, as I mentioned above, containing typographical errors, or missing information.

If a corrected claim is submitted and the insurer still refuses to pay, you can ask for an internal appeal. And if your internal appeal is unsuccessful, you can ask for an external appeal. It's no surprise that the number of health insurance claim and preauthorization denials is huge, as high as 24 percent. The good news is as often as 59 percent of the time that those denials are appealed internally they get reversed; and when an external appeal is needed, up to another 54 percent get reversed and the insurance company pays up![4] In fact, the right to appeal is one of the most important consumer protections added by the Affordable Care Act. (The statistics are on your side, Luiz!).

---

[1] National Retail Federation and the Loss Prevention Research Council.
[2] Creditcards.com.
[3] U.S. Census Bureau.
[4] Government Accountability Office.

CHAPTER 3

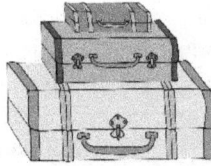

YOUR TRAVEL, TRANSPORTATION, ENTERTAINMENT, AND LIFE'S LITTLE LEGAL LANDMINES

FLYING THE UNFRIENDLY SKIES: What *You* Need to Know About Lost Luggage and the Law

Dear Shari O, My husband Deshaun was on a flight from New York to our home here in Los Angeles. Unbeknownst to me, while in New York, he had bought a beautiful bracelet for me. He still hasn't told me what it cost, but I'm sure it was over $2,000. I'm guessing you already know where I'm going with this…the airline lost his luggage. I'm furious that he didn't put the bracelet in his briefcase and carry it on the plane with him. But the past is the past. What can we do now? Stephanie.

About 2 million pieces of luggage are temporarily or permanently lost each year. That sounds like a lot, but when you consider the amount of luggage airlines move around, it really isn't so bad.

When you buy a flight ticket, you're entering a contract, aka *contract of carriage*, with the airline (airlines are also governed by federal rules and even international treaties). Few of us bother to read the fine print. But here's the thing, if you fly a certain airline often—for example, I fly JetBlue to New York and Washington all the time—I would highly recommend taking the time to print out a copy of the contract of carriage and at least read the sections that you feel are likely to come up for you, which you can easily identify by the section headings. Lost luggage limits will be one of those sections.

In the past, airlines included in their contract of carriage unrealistically low caps for lost, damaged, or delayed luggage, as well as disclaimers for common items everyone knows we all travel with, such as cash, computers, telephones, cameras, and medications. The good news is that a few years ago, our Department of Transportation (DOT) pushed back with "Enhancing Air Passenger Protections" rules addressing things like lengthy tarmac delays, continued delays on chronically late flights, customer service, public access to information, and, yes, liability for losing, damaging, or delaying our luggage. As a result, airlines are responsible for at least $3,300 (adjusted annually for inflation, but always check the current rules as things change) and invalidated many of the exclusions airlines had been trying to get away with.

So, Stephanie, the short answer is to check your airline's contract of carriage for the maximum amount they agreed to pay Deshaun if they lost his luggage. Be sure to carefully follow the airlines claims procedure, which you'll also find in the contract for carriage.

There's no private right of action for violation of the DOT's consumer protection regulations, so you can't sue the airline yourself, and federal law preempts state law when it comes to airline rates, routes, and services. But, if you run into trouble, you can file a report on line with the DOT (www.dot.gov). The DOT can and does fine airlines for refusing to pay legitimate claims.

You didn't ask this question, but a lot of other folks have, so while we're on the subject of airlines legal landmines and ways to stay out of court, don't forget to take a look at what your airline's contract of carriage says about flight delays and cancellations, particularly the airline's obligation to get you on another flight, and pay for your hotel, ground transportation, meals, and incidentals. If your flight's delayed, the DOT now requires airlines to: provide you with a status update every half hour; allow you to get off the plane if the airline decides to open the door, and in any event after three hours; provide snacks and water after two hours; and have operating bathrooms available at all times. If this sounds like basic human requirements, can you imagine what it was like before the DOT stepped in?

When it comes to overbooking and "bumping" you off a flight, your contract of carriage, again, dictates. You may be entitled to cash or check payment, but airlines typically ask for volunteers and offer tickets or vouchers first, sometimes with face values higher than the cash they'd owe you. As a result, especially if you fly an airline often, it may work out better to take the vouchers, which is of course precisely what they're hoping for, but be sure to read the fine print (which often reflects all sorts of restrictions) first.

RENTAL RIP-OFFS: What *You* Need to Know About Car Rental Insurance and the Law

Dear Shari O, My question isn't about a specific thing that happened to me. It's more about whether what rental care agencies tell me all the time is actually true. I travel a lot. It's sort of my thing. And when I travel I love to drive. I've found that it's a great way to really get to know an area. So I'll usually fly into someplace new and rent a car. I don't favor one rental service over another as I've found that one may have the best cars and prices in one area but not another. My question is, they pretty much always recommend that I get insurance coverage, so I do that. Sometimes the insurance is almost as much as the car rental. But a friend recently told me that my own car insurance should cover me. And a co-worker thinks the credit card I use covers me with insurance. Can you tell me if either of them are right? Gabe.

This is a fairly common question we get from traveling drivers.

Your automobile insurance coverage is essentially a contract between you and the insurance carrier. Some of those terms may be dictated by state laws where you live and have purchased the insurance, as some states require certain coverage. Unfortunately, that means there's no easy way to accurately answer this aspect of your question, Gabe, without taking a look at your automobile insurance policy.

In addition to checking to see if, in general, you're covered for an accident that occurs while you're driving a rental car, you'll want to be sure that your automobile insurance policy will cover the costs of damages, specifically, to your own car, the other car, the driver and passengers in your car, the driver and passengers in the other car, and pedestrians. You should also determine whether or not limitations based on fault apply in your state as well as in the states where you will be driving the rental car.

Another set of questions involves whether your own automobile insurance extends to additional drivers of your rental car, as laws vary by state. In New York and California, for example, licensed spouses are generally covered when driving a rental car. You can also list additional drivers on the rental agreement, although most rental companies charge an extra daily fee for this. Be aware that although you've made it clear that your travel in this particular instance is for personal pleasure, Gabe, your regular automobile insurance policy may not cover you when you are renting a car for business use.

As you've also noted, Gabe, many credit cards offer some coverage for rental cars if the card is used to pay for the rental. Again, you'll need to read the terms of your credit card contract. I've seen many credit card contracts that will only cover you for damage to the vehicle you rent. American Express currently offers additional rental car coverage for $15 each time you rent a car. Once you sign up for the service, it's automatic every time you charge a rental car. I know this because I use it.

Your health insurance policy, the terms of which are also dictated by the contract you enter with that provider, will typically also cover injuries that you sustain in a car accident, but will obviously not pay for personal injuries you may cause to another driver, passenger, or pedestrian. And your homeowners or renters insurance may even cover you if possessions are stolen from a rental car…again check your policy.

Finding out the terms and dollar liability caps for your car insurance, credit cards, and health insurance sounds like a lot of work. And it is. Not only that, but if your policies change, you need to verify this information again before you rent each car. That's one reason why some folks just opt to purchase the coverage offered by the rental car companies. But realize that it's wise to make sure you understand the coverage you're getting with that policy as well as the type of situation and damage it covers, what individuals' injuries it will pay for, any dollar caps that apply, and what drivers will be deemed covered.

Here's a quick reference that may help when you're asked to initial the form indicating that you're turning down various types of coverage at the rental car check-out counter:

- Collision Damage: for situations when the rental car is damaged or stolen.

- Supplemental Liability Insurance: typically covers damages to other people's cars and medical costs.

- Personal Accident Insurance: includes medical, ambulance, and death benefits for your injuries and the injuries of your passengers.

- Personal Effects Coverage: covers the theft of your possessions from the rental car.

HOTEL HASSLES: What *You* Need to Know About Overbooked Hotels and the Law

Dear Shari O, My partner and I have created a same-sex, blended family. It hasn't been easy. Both of our ex-husbands have had a hard time dealing with divorce and our "coming out" and have therefore not been easy for us to deal with. And our kids have been struggling with their feelings of loyalty to our ex-husbands and being teased at school, along with the usual adjustments to a new stepparent and stepsiblings. We were finally feeling over the hump so we arranged what we had hoped would be a super-fun family vacation to Nashville. We decided to drive to save money but also because the idea of a road trip sounded like good bonding time. After driving 14 hours, we finally arrived at the hotel, at 11 pm, only to find that the hotel was sold out and had given our room to someone else. They offered to put us up in another hotel, but it was much further away from the attractions we had specifically wanted to be able to walk to. So we wound up finding another hotel on our own for almost twice the price. Now we're trying to get reimbursed for the added cost but they won't even talk to us. Is there anything we can do? Sophia.

When you book a hotel reservation, you are essentially entering into a contract with the hotel. And a confirmed reservation generally equals a *binding contract*, which is why it's important to make sure you get a confirmation number. You'll find disclosures all over the hotel websites to this effect and you will be asked to check a box saying you agree to their cancellation and other policies. Hidden in these policies is their overbooking policy, which almost universally allows hotels to relocate you to a similar hotel if they overbook and sell your room. You'll also typically find language saying they'll only hold your room until a certain time on the check-in day, so if you plan to check in late, one way to avoid this particular legal landmine is to call and e-mail ahead and let the hotel know.

Most states also have specific laws, many dating back to century-old English common law concepts, relevant to hotels (aka *innkeepers*). Back then, weary travelers who reached wayside inns as night approached needed to know they wouldn't be arbitrarily turned away onto the dark roads filled with robbers (or subjected to high prices or deliberately sub-par accommodations that amounted to being turned away).

The very first and most important public duty of a hotel is the duty to receive guests. Hotels are generally liable for damages if they cannot honor a confirmed reservation because of overbooking. Florida's law, for example, makes the hotel responsible for every effort to find alternate accommodations and up to a $500 fine for each guest turned away because of the overbooking.

That's the good news. But back to your question, Sophia. The answer will depend on what the terms you agreed to say, what the applicable state law says, and whether or not the alternative hotel that was offered to you meets the requirements laid out in those two places. My suggestion is that after vetting those two factors, you also check out the rates at the hotel that was offered to you and create a compelling letter explaining why you feel it was not comparable and why the hotel you chose was. My money is on you collecting something, and potentially everything that you reasonably ask for.

The flip side is that hotels can generally sue for damages or retain deposits if you don't show up for a confirmed reservation.

SHIP THIS!: What *You* Need to Know About Cruise Ship Tours and the Law

Dear Shari O, My sister and I just returned from a cruise to Mexico. We had a great time and generally have no complaints. But one tour we signed off for was cancelled. We were required to pay the full $235 per person in advance. Will we be able to get our money back? Beatriz.

The vast majority of cruise excursions are booked through the cruise line itself so I'm going to assume that this was the case with yours, Beatriz.

Much like an airline, when you book yourself on a cruise ship, you're entering a contract with the cruise line. So, for example, claims typically need to be filed in the state indicated on the back of your ticket, regardless of where you live or where in the ocean you were when an event happened. Often that will be Florida, where many of the cruise lines have headquarters. By purchasing the ticket and boarding the ship, you legally consent to these terms, which often include a limited liability waiver and notice-requirement clauses.

My suggestion is to send a letter requesting a refund, following the notification requirements in your ticket, regardless of what your contract says about tour refunds. I've found that as long as the tour was cancelled by the cruise line, they're pretty good about issuing refunds requested in a timely manner.

Something to keep in mind anytime you run into a cruise ship-related legal landmine is that things that happen on a cruise ship, aka a *common carrier*, are handled differently than things that happen on dry land. That's because maritime law, aka *admiralty law*, applies. And most cruise ships serving U.S. customers are not registered in the United States, but rather in countries such as Panama or the Bahamas, where regulations tend to favor the cruise lines. For example, cruise ship contracts generally allow the carrier, for any reason at any time and without prior notice, to cancel, delay, or deviate from any scheduled sailing, port of call, destination, or activity on or off the vessel, or substitute another vessel or port of call, destination, or activity without being liable for any loss, compensation, or refund.

Cruise ship operators still have to exercise *reasonable care* for the safety of their passengers and will be held liable for *negligence* or willful actions.

TICKET TO RIDE: What *You* Need to Know About Phony Event Tickets and the Law

Dear Shari O, I'm writing to you because I am beside myself and just don't know what to do. My fiancée and I just got home from New York City. We'd been planning this trip for months. She is a huge theatre fan. Neither of us make a lot of money so going to New York was a big deal. I spent hours searching online for tickets to see Hamilton *that we would be able to afford and finally found some great seats for $350 each (believe it or not, that's actually a great deal). The seller actually lived in New York so I met him in Times Square on our first day there and paid him cash for the tickets. But when we got to the theatre the next night we were told that the tickets were counterfeit. The usher told us that this happens all the time. Needless to say, my fiancée was crushed and I felt horrible. Now I'm also out $700, which is a lot of money for us. Is there anything I can do? Marty.*

The usher was right, Marty. Sadly, yours is not an uncommon legal landmine, especially for popular in-demand shows and events. Don't kill the messenger, but there's probably not much you can do now, other than to revisit what went wrong and learn from those mistakes.

These scams are all driven by how desirable some tickets have become and how much we're willing to pay for them. Unfortunately, as many as half of the tickets to some events are never even made available to the general public, going instead to insiders or pre-sold, for example, to American Express, to offer to their members as an exclusive. There is, obviously, nothing illegal about doing this. On the other hand, those tickets that are released are often snapped up by ticket bots—software that generally is illegal and that purchases desirable tickets faster than a human could, at rates like 1,000 tickets a minute. The software is used by third-party middlemen who resell the tickets at significant mark-ups and profit, about 49 percent on average, but sometimes over 1,000 percent. Then we've got the lone scammers, like yours, trying to sell phony tickets on places like Craigslist. Especially for red-hot, sold-out tickets like *Hamilton* on Broadway.

Some states are taking more serious steps against the phony ticket scammers—Florida, for example, motivated in part by Disney World, extended its laws to cover its theme parks and new wristband technology. Some of these state laws significantly increase the punishment for people who break the law. The New York Attorney General has also been making a big push recently.

The flip side is that we don't want laws that unfairly impede consumers from legally reselling tickets. Even though tickets have fine print that constitutes a contract and generally says they're non-transferable, most of us consider the tickets we buy to be our own personal property and feel we should be entitled to do whatever we want with them, including reselling. Moreover, we don't want to have to go through certain specified resellers if we want to resell a ticket we buy. So it's a bit of a slippery slope.

With that in mind, if you are going to buy a ticket from Craigslist or another similar source that's not a designated ticket reseller, there are some things you can do to protect yourself from scams like this in the future, Marty. For example, ask for a copy of the seller's invoice proving that the tickets have been paid for, check the venue's website to verify they're actually for a seat and concert date and time that exists, meet the seller in a safe public place in person, ask to see ID, and pay with a check or PayPal.

VILLAINOUS VALETS: What *You* Need to Know About Valet Parking and the Law

Dear Shari O, Our favorite Italian restaurant offers free valet parking. We've been going there, and letting the valet guys park our car, for years without incident. When this past weekend we ate there, the valet parked our car as usual, we had a great meal and came home. But the next morning my wife went to the Apple store to have her iPad, which she had left in the back seat of the car, looked at and it wasn't there. She put it there just before we went out to dinner, so we know it had to go missing while we were at the restaurant. I left a voice message at the restaurant this morning, but I want to be prepared and know my rights when they call me back. What are my rights here? Madison.

Most of us assume that valet providers are as driven to provide us with as good service as the restaurant, hotel, or other venue where they're parking cars, and that they are required to reimburse us for a stolen car or items stolen from our car while it's in their possession. But that's because most of us have never read the fine print on valet tickets and the signs they typically post, aka our *contract*, with the valet provider. While the degree of responsibility assumed varies from one valet service to another, most do their best to limit their responsibility.

Unfortunately, these terms almost always provide that any damage must be reported to the valet company before you leave the parking premises. This requirement makes sense since any number of things can happen to your car and its possessions once you leave the parking lot and, if not for this requirement, it would be easy for folks to blame these things on valet companies.

In your case, Madison, it sounds as if you lack proof that the iPad was in the car in the first place, may have ignored the warnings on the valet signs and your parking ticket, left the premises before making a claim, and, thus, in all likelihood cannot prove who stole your wife's iPad. As a result, it's not likely you will be able to collect unless the restaurant owner appreciates your business and just wants to be a nice guy.

That doesn't mean that valet companies, in general, have no responsibility. Valet companies are required by law to use a *reasonable standard of care* when hiring and training employees, as well as in how they handle their parking lots, your car, and car keys. Valet companies are also required to follow state and federal laws, including labor laws. For example, it's generally mandatory that valet companies check their employees' driving records, references, and employment history. And the National Valet Parking

Association requires their members to adhere to certain security measures, including measures to prevent vehicle theft. For example, valet companies are advised to lock the doors of all cars kept in their company and secure car keys in a locked box. Of course, these laws and requirements are not always followed, which can make a difference if you wind up with a legal landmine involving a valet parking company. Knowing, for example, that the company did not properly vet its employees can provide you with negotiating leverage and help your case.

The list of things that can possibly go wrong when we valet park our cars is quite extensive: your car can be stolen, given to the wrong person or damaged; you can be personally injured by a car being parked, relocated, or retrieved; your private information can be accessed via insurance or other documents left in your car (even addresses saved in your car's navigation system are vulnerable) and misused; your keys, remotes, and access cards left in your car can be duplicated, putting your home at risk; and your car can be taken for an unauthorized joy ride or, worse yet, injure someone. As a result, getting into the habit of taking routine precautions to avoid these legal landmines makes sense.

Here are some suggestions.

Don't leave valuable items in your car. Remove remote controls, keys, documents, and other personal items. If your car comes with a valet key that starts the ignition and opens the driver's side door but prevents the valet from gaining access to valuables in your trunk and glove box, use it. Ensure that the person to whom you're handing your keys actually is a valet driver. Take a moment to eyeball the terms you're agreeing to on the back of your valet ticket. Look your car over before the valet takes it and keep an eye out as the car is parked. And, when you get it back, look it over again before leaving. Is anything missing? Has the car been damaged in any way?

If something is wrong, the first rule of thumb is to *never leave the premises*. Again, most valet tickets clearly state they accept no responsibility once you leave the premises. Ask to speak with a manager. Find out who owns the valet company and parking lot and what their relationship is with the restaurant or other business they're parking cars for. Make sure you get the name of anyone who drove or was in your car. You may later be able to show, for example, that the driver did not have a valid driver's license or was inexperienced. If your car was damaged, photograph the space your car was parked in and any surrounding cars. These are issues that may point driver liability back at the valet company owner. Depending on the extent of damage and your sense of whether you're going to get cooperation, you may want to call the police to file a report at this time, too. While you're waiting, take photos of the damage and of any signs, tickets, or other disclosures in sight. Ask other customers and employees for contact information so they can serve as witnesses. Look for security cameras—if any are present, you may want to ask to see the tape. Ask for a claims form and the valet company's insurance carrier and don't leave until you have written acknowledgment.

TOO HOT TO HANDLE: What *You* Need to Know About Restaurant Food Liability and the Law

Dear Shari O, Our extended family celebrated my folks' 50th wedding anniversary last month. As a special treat, my wife and I took everyone out to dinner at one of my parents' favorite steakhouses. My mom is a big fan of their spinach artichoke dip so we ordered a few of those for the table. They must heat it up in a microwave because when my son bit into some on a chip, he let out a scream, spit it out, and grabbed a glass of water. The dip actually caused second-degree burns in his mouth. The waiter was very apologetic. I've written a letter to the restaurant manager-owner asking for $450 for my son's doctor visit and his pain, suffering, and inconvenience, which I feel is very fair. But I haven't heard back and am now thinking I may need to call and get a little more aggressive. What are my legal rights here? Kerry.

As is the case when you stay in a hotel, Kerry, you're allowed to have certain reasonable expectations about the safety of the food you're fed in a restaurant. And the restaurant has a responsibility to meet that *standard of care*—in other words, to not be unreasonably *negligent* in the way it handles the food it feeds you. That generally means maintaining a safe environment, producing safe meals, and eliminating unreasonable dangers.

As is always the case with negligence, you will need to prove that the restaurant's negligence, in this case overheating your son's food, caused the injury to him. By going directly to the doctor's office, it sounds as if you have done what you need to document the negligence. Statements from the waiter and family members who were there may also help.

Depending on how serious the injury is, you may be able to ask for medical bills and other out-of-pocket expenses, pain and suffering, emotional distress, and even lost income. The bottom line: what you're asking here is not unreasonable.

Food poisoning cases, which is not the issue here but is the legal landmine that comes up often with restaurants, are more difficult to pursue. That's because symptoms often materialize later and negligence is not always as easy to prove, since you may not know which food you ate actually caused the problem. That's why, in those cases, the proof is often having several people who ate the same thing on the same day complain.

Restaurants may also be found *strictly liable* for a defective food product. A *product liability* claim means that the food was not suitable for consumption. Some states have strict liability rules, meaning all you need to show is that the food was contaminated and made you sick. You don't need to show that the restaurant did anything wrong to cause the illness.

Another legal approach might be *breach of warranty*. That would either be an *implied* warranty (in other words, the restaurant failed to meet minimum standards required of the food), or an *explicit* warranty if, for example, the restaurant advertised that its food was washed three times for added safety.

My instinct tells me that this is a case in which you will be reimbursed, but that you are correct, you may need to get more aggressive. And don't forget to document, document, document.

FOLLOW THAT CAB!: What You Need to Know About Taxicab Driver Liability and the Law

Dear Shari O, I went to the most awesome party at my fraternity house last weekend. The problem is that I took a taxicab back to my dorm and accidentally left my brand-new winter coat in the cab. Of course I didn't realize it until the next morning. Is there anything I can legally do to get my coat back? Isabel.

Because they carry passengers for a fee, taxicabs are considered *common carriers*. As such, both the drivers and owners of taxicabs owe their passengers the highest degree of duty of care when it comes to their driving. The taxicab business is also subject to a plethora of state regulations including inspections, testing, permitting, licensing, and franchising. When it comes to liability for your personal items, on the other hand, passengers are generally deemed to have assumed that responsibility. Given the number of passengers that are in and out of a given taxicab each day, this makes sense, as any number of things can happen to personal items left behind.

We see variations in the forms of ownership amongst taxicabs, which can potentially be relevant should a legal landmine arise. In some cases, cab drivers own their cabs, so they're solely responsible for what happens in their taxicab, which includes lost items, accidents, you name it. In other cases, taxi drivers merely rent the cab from the owner, in which case both the driver and the taxicab company may be liable for these events. In still other cases, taxicab companies own the vehicles and employ drivers directly, putting the cab company on the hook.

Then there's the common sense aspect. Smaller towns tend to have fewer cab companies and are run by individuals who tend to behave more like small-town residents. And if you can describe the cab or even recall what company it was or kept the receipt, you can probably call the local cab companies, narrow down the driver, and get your coat back. In larger urban areas, that is virtually impossible. In cities like New York, for example, if you have a receipt you may be in luck. You can call the dispatcher who can hopefully reach the driver and make arrangements to get you your coat. But if you don't know the company, cab, or driver, your only option is to file a report with every police precinct and cab company, which can be time-consuming and frankly a waste of time.

So Isabel, whether you'll ever see your beloved coat again depends in large part on where you go to college and the strength of your memory.

HEALTH CLUB HAVOC: What *You* Need to Know About Gym Memberships and the Law

Dear Shari O, When I started college this past fall I joined the gym downstairs in my building. A trainer walked me around and showed me the equipment and facilities. And I could have sworn he said there was personal training and other perks included. But it turned out that there was an extra fee for everything. And I wound up hardly ever using the gym. I've been trying to cancel my membership for over a month now and keep getting the runaround. I thought about just not paying the monthly fee anymore. What should I do? Connor.

As we've discussed with many other situations, Connor, the agreement you sign with a gym is a *contract*, so contract law governs (except in the case of injury and other situations where tort law often applies—see below).

Gym membership contracts can be tricky, because you're often asked to sign on the fly, without much time to actually read the fine print. And there can be quite a lot of fine print, much of which has nothing to do with the things you care about, such as how long the pool is open or the type of free weights they use. Instead, many gym contracts include legal fine print covering things like early cancellation fees and waivers of liability, which tends to be how the legal landmines arise.

So your first task, Connor, is to check and see what your contract says about cancelling. Oftentimes, cancelling a gym membership is allowed with payment of a fee and provision of notice. If so, that's typically the easiest and cheapest route, but be sure to follow the fine print exactly to avoid having your gym claim you didn't cancel correctly and have to start the process all over again.

If your contract doesn't not allow for cancellation, all is not lost. In many cases I've come across, the gym has done something that wasn't completely above-board—for example, the individual who sold the membership made material misrepresentations of fact that caused a customer to enter into a contract. It sounds like that may be the case here, Connor, if you were told things that turned out not to be true. While that may be difficult to prove, if the same person told other members similar things, management may notice a trend and be more likely to believe you.

Another situation I've encountered is contract terms that are clearly unfair, illegal, unconscionable, or against public policy—for example, a contract that provides for automatic renewal without your permission, or allows the gym to significantly change the facilities or the contract price. We see these unfair provisions a lot less frequently now because federal and state governments have investigated abusive practices, and now just about every state has specific regulations setting limits on what terms are acceptable in gym membership contracts. If your contract does not comply, it is likely unenforceable.

Most state regulations also allow you to cancel at any time in certain circumstances, such as disability or death, if you move more than a certain number of miles from the facility and cannot transfer the contract to a comparable facility, or if the facility ceases to offer the services listed in your contract. And there are generally short periods after you sign a membership contract during which you can cancel.

If you find that you're out of options to cancel, you may want to request a temporary membership freeze period, which I've found most will agree to. College students who travel elsewhere for the summer often do this.

As is often the case when it comes to life's little legal landmines, an ounce of prevention is worth a pound of cure. That means reading your contract up front and addressing any language that may become a problem...or finding another gym. Smaller community gyms tend to be more flexible if you see something in the contract you want to change. They also tend to be easier to cancel because you can often ask to speak with the actual owner. And when it comes to just not paying, smaller gyms are less likely to go after you for the balance due under your contract. The larger chains, on the other hand, will likely not be willing to change anything in their form contract, can be very difficult when it comes to cancelling, and will almost certainly sell your unpaid debt to a debt collection agency, which can be a nightmare. Based on the facts you've provided, I am going to assume you're dealing with a larger chain gym and I generally recommend against your idea of just not paying.

CHAPTER 4

NEGOTIATING SETTLEMENTS 101

In the context of life's little legal landmines, negotiation is essentially communication between multiple parties in order to reach an agreement that all can live with and that all perceive as better, overall, than other available options.

These notions may translate to more legwork, thought, and preparation for negotiating a settlement and avoiding small claims court than first meets the eye. Among other things, as the definition I've provided for you above suggests, anticipating and meeting at least some of the other side's needs is imperative for a negotiation to succeed in terms of reaching a settlement. Sometimes, more than one attempt at negotiation will be needed. You cannot control the manner in which the other side handles himself, but by handling yourself well, even a negotiation that does not conclude with an actual settlement can be helpful in terms of establishing your credibility, educating the other side about the merits of your position and the flaws in his, and building rapport.

Assessment

All things being equal, the side that does the best job at pre-negotiation information-gathering and assessment wins. For that reason, assessment is often the most important and time-consuming part of the negotiating process. I can pretty much guarantee you that there are facts waiting to be found that will make a difference in the outcome of your negotiations— facts that will help you determine not only how much the other guy is willing to cough up, but how to motivate him to settle. For example, suppose the other side is worried that once word gets out about your settlement, other customers may come after him too; you're going to have to address that concern if you want to settle. Most folks start out overestimating their own options, leverage, and acceptable terms, and underestimating the other side's. The more realistic and accurate you can get during this pre-negotiation assessment phase, the more likely your negotiation will succeed.

Initial pre-assessment questions you can ask yourself:

- What are your other realistically available options and what other options are realistically available to the other side?

- What type of settlement could you live with and what do you believe the other side can grow to accept?

- What leverage do you and the other side have?

- Can you or the other side prove the legal elements needed to win in court if necessary?

- Does the other side realize your strong legal position?

Just as important as pre-assessing your negotiating position is the need to assess what it is that you are really trying to achieve. For example, oftentimes plaintiffs (the ones doing the suing) want to be made whole, and defendants (the ones getting sued) believe they've been falsely accused and want their reputations restored. If your goal is to "teach that guy a lesson," please put down this book and stop wasting your time. Not only does a motivation like that decrease the likelihood that you are going to be able to settle, but you're not going to be able to teach him a lesson. If he's reached this point in life and his parents, siblings, friends, teachers, spouse, and kids couldn't do it, you certainly will not. And suing someone is an awfully expensive way to teach a person you don't really care all that much about a lesson. Only once in my entire 30-year legal career did I have a client who could actually afford to do that, and even he settled.

Likewise, if your goal is for the other side to see that you were "right," step away from this book. Sure, there are some real bad guys out there. But oftentimes, the legal landmine arose because things just didn't go as planned or there was a misunderstanding between two not-so-bad individuals, who've both since rationalized their behaviors, and who both now feel victimized. Because you're only human, the level of your emotional investment is directly inversely related to your ability to think rationally. Most legal professionals will tell you that ego, pride, and self-righteousness are the mortal enemies of settlement. Which leads us to the tone of your communication and demeanor.

Communication and Demeanor

Think about the type of request or suggestions that you are most open to. If you're like most of us, you respond well to someone who pleasantly looks you in the eye and, in a friendly or at least non-emotive tone, politely asks for something you consider to be reasonable and appropriate, or at least not completely nuts. Folks who won't look us in the eye, or blast us with threatening demands or ridiculous expectations…not so much.

Moreover, research indicates as much as 50 percent of our communication is non-verbal. During your communications, keep in mind that the other guy may be trying to read your facial expression, tone of voice, or body language. Or maybe you can read into his expression, tone, or body language.

The Ask

Most of us learned as children that one of the best ways to get something we want is to ask for it. Negotiating a settlement is no different. At some point, you're going to have to ask.

The "ask" can take different forms: communication between parties with an ongoing relationship will likely be verbal, and communication between parties who don't really know each other will likely be in writing (aka a *demand letter*). Oftentimes, various forms of communication will be available to you, each with its specific advantages and disadvantages. For example, it may benefit you to allow the other side time to digest an offer prior to feeling the urge to respond. A written offer is more suitable for this scenario. Particularly when it comes to the actual ask, think about whether to make an offer face-to-face or by letter, email, telephone, or during mediation.

For in-person meetings, think about location and how you might leverage that to your advantage. For example, individuals tend to feel more comfortable in their own offices, but tend to be less demanding in other locations where they're less comfortable.

Consider the order of issues addressed. Some of the most successful negotiators I've worked with tend to lead with the indisputable facts and build around them, emphasizing the strongest main points first and last. A common mistake you'll want to avoid is succumbing to the urge to talk about every detail of the other side's actions you feel were wrong. The problem is that when you do that, your actual credible points wind up getting lost in the minutia and the parties may wind up bickering over points that don't really matter. So it's always best to stick with your one or two main points, and remember, you're going to have to address the other side's strongest arguments, too.

Finally, there's the question of who makes the first offer. Research indicates that, as long as you know what your goal is and have done your homework, there is no correlation between who makes the first offer and the outcome. Opening offers tend to fall into one of three buckets: a fair opening offer, a slightly unreasonable opening offer, or a completely unreasonable opening offer. Studies indicate that the only time you will get the best result with a completely unreasonable opening offer is if the other person is very motivated to settle. In other cases, a slightly unreasonable offer may be best.

The Back-and-Forth

Since its highly unlikely that the other side will simply agree to your first offer right out of the box, or vice versa, your negotiation's bound to involve some back-and-forth communication. This stage may occur between the parties or it may occur in mediation (see below), but the strategies remain the same.

I've often seen clients become frustrated with this stage of negotiation. But remember, each back-and-forth communication presents another opportunity to acquire knowledge and knowledge is power. Negotiation power goes to those who listen and learn. So it's important to ask questions and get as much relevant information as you can throughout this stage of the process. There are two basic types of information: *substantive facts*, such as the other's side's perspective on who, what, when, and where, which can be proven by documents, e-mails, witnesses, and such; and *motivational facts*, including the other person's goals and objectives, motives, fears, concerns, and interests. For example, if the other side is short on cash, it may behoove you to offer a payment schedule. Since leverage is situational, and information is power, be aware that the other side may be trying to gather information from you as well. Throughout this process, consider selective information-sharing in order to persuade the other side to settle. It is important to be deliberate about what information to disclose, what information to avoid disclosing, and when disclosures should occur.

Assuming you have a good case and the other side knows it, confidence in your case and your willingness to go to court if needed is a strong leverage point for you and should certainly be established. However, beginners often make the fatal mistake of trying to aggressively convince the other side of the merits of their case. Doing so is a waste of time as the other side's going to be doing the same thing to you in order to establish their leverage and save face. Instead, focus on getting information, building rapport, asking questions, and probing the other side's needs, concerns, and options. Balancing these two seemingly disparate points—that you have full confidence in the merits of your case, but still want to settle—is perhaps the most difficult dynamic in any negotiation. Establishing and then maintaining your credibility throughout the process is key.

Leverage, like credibility, is an advantage that can shift if the other party gathers information or sees through your strengths. It is always best to reach a settlement while your leverage and credibility is strong.

The perception of fairness is also key in negotiations. You can create this perception, and increase your own credibility, by referencing appropriate objective standards with your counter-offers. Examples include comparable products, market value, precedent, or expert opinion. If both sides can agree on fair and reasonable standards that are applicable to what the settlement amount should be, your negotiation is more likely to succeed.

Another key element requires ensuring that the other side walks away feeling like he negotiated a good deal. There are many ways to accomplish this, but one of the more common methods is to always leave room to come up in your offers so the other side continually feels as if he has won something.

Post Negotiation

When maintaining a relationship after the negotiation is important to both sides, problem-solving negotiation may be a better alternative for you than more traditional adversarial negotiation. Briefly, each side more transparently lists their needs and wants, compares them, and then searches for win-win solutions together. The goal is finding an outcome that serves as many of each of the sides' interests as possible. Studies show problem-solving is more likely to succeed when a mutually respected independent third party is present.

The really good news is that individuals who negotiate and enter a settlement agreement on their own accord are far more likely to pay the sum they agree to pay than those who lose a lawsuit and are ordered to pay by a judge—so you will not likely need to worry about collecting.

CHAPTER 5

EVERYTHING YOU NEED TO KNOW ABOUT MEDIATION

Mediation is a process often used to resolve disputes. You'll find countless books dedicated entirely to the topic of mediation. But I'm guessing you have no interest in becoming an expert on the subject. So I'm only going to cover the basics that you really need to know in the context of trying to settle life's little legal landmines.

There are a lot of reasons you might want to try mediation as an option for resolving your legal landmine before thinking about going to court. For starters, mediation is typically a lot quicker, cheaper, and less formal, meaning less of a learning curve, less time and far less stress. That's because rather than filing your case with the court and having to wait your turn for a court date along with everyone else, you can get the mediation ball rolling by simply agreeing to try it with the other side and finding a qualified mediator (which you can easily do online or from referrals). Not only do mediators cost a lot less than lawyers, but it's normal to split the cost with the other side.

What Qualifies a Mediator?

In a nutshell, a mediator is a professional trained as a neutral party to help people embroiled in a dispute reach a mutually agreeable compromise. Oftentimes, mediators may also be lawyers, retired judges, licensed therapists, or professional educators, but not always.

Each state has its own guidelines for certifying mediators. Most require a minimum amount of education, certification classroom time, and experience, as well as periodic re-certification. Many states also offer specialty certifications.

In addition to mandatory licensing qualifications, you'll want to select a mediator, at a minimum, based on her experience with cases similar to yours, her reputation, and her hourly rate.

Mediators do not provide counseling or legal advice. Instead, as a neutral party, a good mediator will help you and the other side focus on solving your dispute. She may talk you through the facts and legal elements of your case, pointing out weaknesses and suggesting how they might be perceived by a judge in order to help you both see the actual realistic and most likely ways your case might play out—and help you decide if you're better off settling or not.

You can prepare for a mediation in much the same way you prepare for a negotiation. Your mediation will begin with the mediator introducing herself and the role she'll play and explaining the process. Typically she'll then ask both sides to explain what happened and give their perspectives of the case. It is then not unusual for her to alternate between meeting with both parties together and then with each side separately and in private (aka *to caucus*), discussing facets she feels will help resolve differences. A mediator is prohibited from sharing information you discuss during a private caucus with the other side unless you tell her she can. Mediations can last from a few hours to several days, depending on the complexity of the dispute and how much the parties are willing to invest in trying to resolve it amicably. They generally end when the parties reach an agreement on some or all of the issues and sign an agreement, or when one or both parties agree they cannot reach an agreement (aka an *impasse*).

As a certified mediator myself, I love mediations because they're private and, with a few exceptions, are required by law to be kept confidential by both parties. This allows everyone an opportunity to come to the table for a far more candid discussion than in a courtroom, which can increase the likelihood of reaching a compromise. In that sense, some lawyers view mediations as a great way to acquire important information about the other side's case and mindset. I prefer to express the strength of mediations less contentiously, instead seeing them as a way to better understand each other. But it is a point worth noting if there is important information you want to keep close to your chest. In contrast, once you file a lawsuit, and especially if you engage a lawyer, the parties often tend to become more invested in litigating and there may be too many opinions and personal agendas to compromise.

Because folks tend to feel more in control, payments promised in mediation agreements are more likely to be made without collection hassles than payments a judge dictates a party to make in a court order. I've also seen many instances where we appear to have an impasse, only to have one or both parties reach out afterwards with some kind of a settlement offer.

APPENDIX

LEGAL CONCEPTS AND THEIR 'ELEMENTS'

The following is a quick recap of some of the more common legal landmines and the elements required to prove them in court. Knowing the extent to which you can or cannot prove the elements in your case can provide you with essential negotiating leverage or, conversely, motivation to settle.

Negligent Tort
- Duty
- Breach
- Caused damage

Intentional Tort
- Duty
- Breach
- Intent to breach
- Caused damage

Strict Liability Tort
- Inherently dangerous or unreasonable act or omission or relation
- Caused injury and damage

Product Liability
- Manufacturer duty
- Breach (defective product)
- Used product as intended
- Caused injury and damage

Nuisance
- Unreasonable interference for unreasonable time
- Causation
- Damage

Trespass
- Unlawful unauthorized entry
- Intent
- Force

- Damage

Conversion
- Clear ownership or right to possess
- Intent to use or possess for self
- Wrongful disposition of property right
- Caused damage

Tortious Interference
- Contractual or beneficial business relationship
- Knowledge of relationship
- Intent to induce breach in relationship
- Lack of privilege to induce breach
- Breach of relationship
- Caused damage

Conspiracy
- Agreement
- Intent to carry out unlawful act of by unlawful means
- Overt act in furtherance

Fraud
- Intentional knowing misrepresentation of material fact
- With intent to deceive victim to rely
- Reasonable reliance
- Caused damage

Negligent Misrepresentation
- False statement of material fact with no reason to believe it was true
- Intent to induce reliance
- Reasonable reliance
- Caused damage

Defamation (Libel if written, Slander if spoken)
- False statement of fact
- Publication
- At least without reason to believe factually correct (in matters of public concern, actual malice—knowledge of falsity—may be required)

- Caused damage (in some states assumed per se)

Battery
- Unauthorized act
- Intent to harm or offend
- Harmful or offensive contact

Assault
- Unauthorized act
- Intended to cause apprehension of harmful or offensive contact
- That causes such apprehension

False Imprisonment
- Intent
- Detention, confinement, or restraint absent consent
- Cause
- Awareness

Invasion of Privacy
- Intrusion into solitude or private affairs
- Public disclosure of embarrassing private information
- Publicity putting into public false light
- Appropriation of name or photo for personal or commercial advantage

Intentional Infliction of Emotional Distress
- Outrageous conduct
- Intent to cause distress, or recklessly causing distress, that adversely impacts mental health
- Caused damage

ABOUT THE AUTHOR

Shari Africk-Olefson was born in New York where her grandparents, Dave and Alma Siegler and Benjamin and Lillian Olefson, played a huge role in her upbringing. Dave, a New York City fireman, and Ben, who owned a Kosher butcher shop in Harlem, helped instill in Shari a solid work ethic and life-long passion for helping others. The family relocated to Florida when Shari was just ten years old.

Shari graduated from Pine Crest School in 1981 and then Carnegie Mellon University where she double-majored in Journalism and Psychology. From there, it was off to New York City and Yeshiva University's law school, then earning an LLM (Master of Law Degree) in Finance, Development and Real Property from the University of Miami.

Shari began her legal career as an intern with the Broward County, Florida Public Defender's office. She practiced law for several years before being recruited by a Fortune 300 company to run a joint venture. In 2006, Shari began writing her first book, *Foreclosure Nation: Mortgaging the American Dream* (Prometheus, 2009), to be soon followed by *Foreclosure Defense Strategies* (Aspatore, 2009), *Foreclosures: What Lawyers Need to Know Now* (Andrews Publications, 2009), *Structuring Commercial Real Estate Transactions* (Thompson Reuters, 2010), *Financial Fresh Start* (AMACOM, 2012) aka *The Great American Do-Over*. At around the same time, Shari was invited to appear on various South Florida news stations as a subject matter expert covering our horrific foreclosure crisis. Local segments lead to regular segments on national television and radio including CNBC, Fox News, MSNCB, CBS, PBS, NPR, CNN, CSPAN, Yahoo!, and Bloomberg. Eventually, NBC affiliate WPTV and Fox 29 engaged Shari in a regular weekly "Consumer Help" segment, to which she continues to dedicate her time today, providing important public interest, legal, and mental health news and information.

A member of the Florida, District of Columbia, and New York Bar Associations and a Florida Bar Certified Real Estate Specialist, Shari has worked for prominent law firms handling complex transactions and managing foreclosing litigation, as a Civil Circuit-Supreme Court Certified Mediator, expert witness, and as Director of The Carnegie Group, a non-partisan think tank providing awareness, education, and advocacy as well as consumer-facing content, subject matter experts, and independent third-party validation in the real estate, finance, legal, and healthcare industries for clients including the National Association of Realtors and Freddie Mac, as well as non-profit, trade, government, and financial institutions.

In 2012, Shari founded the nonprofit Women's Equal Pay Network, dedicated to championing workplace equality and legal justice for women by providing a safe space for women experiencing workplace bias to tell their stories, connect with others, get empowered, and eliminate the stigma associated with speaking out. And more recently, Shari returned to college to earn her Masters of Psychology degree from Nova Southeastern University.

Shari was motivated to write *101 Ways To Stay Out of Court* because she realizes how difficult going to court can be for folks and knows that sometimes just a little bit of information and guidance can make a world of difference.